STUDY GUIDE AND CASEBOOK FOR MANAGERIAL ECONOMICS

SEVENTH EDITION

Study Guide and Casebook for Managerial Economics

SEVENTH EDITION

by

Edwin Mansfield
late of the University of Pennsylvania

Thomas Donley
DePaul University

Henry R. Hertzfeld
George Washington University

W. W. Norton & Company
New York   London

W. W. Norton & Company has been independent since its founding in 1923, when William Warder Norton and Mary D. Herter Norton first published lectures delivered at the People's Institute, the adult education division of New York City's Cooper Union. The firm soon expanded its program beyond the Institute, publishing books by celebrated academics from America and abroad. By mid-century, the two major pillars of Norton's publishing program—trade books and college texts—were firmly established. In the 1950s, the Norton family transferred control of the company to its employees, and today—with a staff of four hundred and a comparable number of trade, college, and professional titles published each year—W. W. Norton & Company stands as the largest and oldest publishing house owned wholly by its employees.

Ancillaries Editor: Rachel Comerford
Manufacturing by the Courier Companies—Westford, MA
Book design by Jack Meserole
Production manager: Benjamin Reynolds
Composition and project management by the Westchester Book Group/Debbie Masi

ISBN: 978-0-393-93396-3 (pbk.)

W. W. Norton & Company, Inc., 500 Fifth Avenue, New York, N.Y. 10110

www.wwnorton.com

W. W. Norton & Company Ltd., Castle House, 75/76 Wells Street, London W1T 3QT

1 2 3 4 5 6 7 8 9 0

Contents

Preface

This *Study Guide and Casebook* is designed to supplement *Managerial Economics*, seventh edition. A major feature of the seventh edition of this *Study Guide* is that it contains the following six full-length classroom-tested cases: (1) How H-P Used Tactics of the Japanese to Beat Them at Their Game (*Wall Street Journal*), (2) A Managerial Application of Cost Functions by a Railroad (by Edwin Mansfield and Harold Wein), (3) Déjà vu: The Internet and Past Innovations (by Michael Totty), (4) CATCO Electronics Corporation (USA) (by Patrick Schul, William Cunningham, and Lynn Gill), (5) How Technology Tailors Price Tags (*Wall Street Journal*), and (6) The Carriage House Inn: A Family Corporation (by Michael Everett). We are grateful to these authors and publications for permission to reprint their cases here. Each chapter of this book parallels closely the contents of the corresponding chapter of the text. In order to provide comprehensive and varied exercises and problems, a five-pronged approach has been adopted:

1. *Chapter profiles* highlight and summarize the principal points of the chapter in the text.

2. An easy-to-read digest of selected *significant formulas* from the chapters in the text.

3. Limbering-up exercises in the form of *completion questions* open the way to systematic review of each chapter.

4. Self-tests in the form of *true or false* and *multiple choice* questions are provided.

5. A considerable number of *problems* are taken up. These problems often simulate real-world situations and require the student to work with actual data in tabular and diagrammatic form.

Answers to all the questions and problems are contained at the end of each chapter.

This book contains over 500 questions and problems, enough to provide the student with a thorough review. Since a study guide should be a flexible learning tool, an attempt was made to supply not only a large number of questions but also a wide range in terms of difficulty. Each chapter begins at a relatively easy level, increasing gradually in rigor as students build confidence along with competence. The more demanding an economic concept, the more extensive the amount of review material given to it. Some of the problems at the end of chapters are hard enough that the typical student should not expect to answer them all. Even the best students should be challenged by some of them.

Edwin Mansfield
Thomas Donley
Henry R. Hertzfeld

Part One
THE NEED FOR A GUIDE

CHAPTER 1

Introduction

Chapter Profile

Managerial economics uses formal models to analyze the actions of managers and the effect of those actions on organizations. In contrast to microeconomics, which is largely focused on firms and markets, managerial economics is focused on behavior. Courses in managerial economics provide fundamental analytical tools to help guide managers make better decisions. Managerial economics recognizes the complexity of the world and helps students learn to integrate the many factors essential for good management and think about the long-term consequences of decision making.

For both nonbusiness organizations and firms, the process of decision making can be divided into five basic steps: (1) Establish or identify the organization's objectives. (2) Define the problem. (3) Identify possible solutions. (4) Select the best possible solution. (5) Implement the solution.

To apply managerial economics to business management, we need a theory of the firm. Most managers make decisions aimed at increasing the value of their organization. The theory for a profit-oriented firm defines this as maximizing the present value of the organization's expected future cash flows.

Managerial economists define **profits** somewhat differently than do accountants. When economists speak of profit, they mean profit over and above what the owners' labor and capital employed in the business could earn elsewhere. To a considerable extent, the differences between the concept of profit used by accountants and that used by economists reflect the differences in their functions.

Profits (and losses) are the mainsprings of a free-enterprise economy. They are signals that indicate where resources are needed and where they are too abundant. They are important incentives for making choices that may involve risk, and they are society's reward for efficiency. Managers can also earn profit by exploiting market inefficiencies to give their firm a sustainable competitive advantage.

Although managerial economists generally assume that firms want to maximize profit, they recognize additional goals that managers may wish to achieve. Some of these goals may enhance the firm's long-term value, whereas others may only reflect the managers' desire to increase their own compensation, particularly when the managers are not the owners of the firm. The latter is called the principal–agent problem, and there are incentives such as stock option plans that owners can provide to managers in order to give managers a financial stake in the firm's future success.

Every market has a demand side and a supply side. The market demand curve shows the amount of a product that buyers would be willing and able to purchase at various prices. The market supply curve shows the amount of a product that sellers would be willing and able to offer at various prices. The equilibrium price is the price where the quantity demanded equals the quantity supplied—and is the point where the market will tend to return if, at any given time, the actual price is not equal to the equilibrium price.

Changing factors underlying the consumer's demand for a product can shift the demand curve, just as changing factors related to the cost of producing a product can shift the supply curve. Understanding these factors is a key element in making good managerial decisions.

Key Formulas to Remember

1. Present value of expected future profits:

$$PV = \sum_{t=1}^{n} \frac{\pi_t}{(1 + i)^t}$$

or, because profits = total revenue (TR) minus total cost (TC),

$$PV = \sum_{t=1}^{n} \frac{TR_t - TC_t}{(1 + i)^t}$$

where $\pi = TR - TC$, t = time, and i = interest rate.

2. The demand function is downward-sloping:

$Q_D = a - bP$ (for the case of a straight-line demand curve)

where a is the intercept, b is the slope of the curve, and P is the price of the product.

3. The supply function is upward-sloping:

$Q_S = a + bP$ (has a positive, or upward-sloping, shape)

4. Equilibrium:

$$Q_D = Q_S$$

where Q_D is quantity demanded, and Q_S is quantity supplied.

Questions

Wool: An Opening Example

Because this is an introductory chapter, we do not present the full range of questions that will be included in subsequent chapters of this study guide. We begin by considering an interesting and important example—the case of wool.

(a) During the late 1980s, wool prices increased considerably, due in part to increased demand by China and the former Soviet Union. From 1977 to 1988, the price of wool for worsted clothing rose from $3.67 to $5.81 per pound. Expecting that wool prices would remain high, wool producers raised a lot more sheep. Did this result in a shift to the right in the supply curve for wool? Why or why not?

(b) At the same time, the Chinese and Russians cut back on their purchases of wool because of the lack of foreign currency (and in the case of China, because of organizational problems). Did this shift the demand curve for wool to the left? Why or why not?

(c) Australia is the world's largest producer of wool, and for a time the Australian Wool Corporation propped up the price of wool by buying up unsold Australian wool. Why was this necessary to prevent the price from falling?

(d) The Australian Wool Corporation had to buy up so much wool that it exhausted its cash reserves and its credit. The firm turned for help to the Australian government, but its parliament refused to guarantee further loans to buy up more surplus wool. In March 1991, the actual price of wool fell to about $2.50 per pound. Why?

True or False

_____   1. Firms' managers will always work to maximize profits.

_____   2. An action that increases today's profits will increase a firm's value.

_____   3. If actual price exceeds equilibrium price, there is a tendency for actual price to rise.

_____   4. A shift to the right of the market supply curve tends to increase the equilibrium price.

_____   5. In any market, the seller alone determines the price of the product that is bought and sold. Because the seller has the product, and the buyer does not have it, the buyer must pay what the seller asks.

Multiple Choice

1. Suppose that the market demand curve and the market supply curve for broccoli are as shown in the following graph.

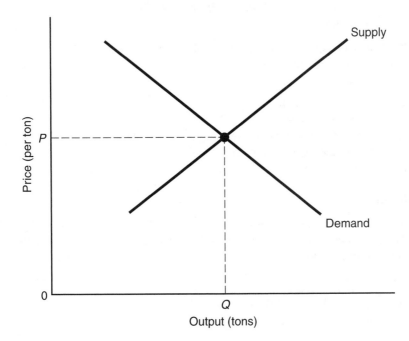

If the government sets a price greater than the equilibrium price, the result will be:

    a.   a reduction in the quantity of broccoli supplied
    b.   an excess supply of broccoli
    c.   a shift to the right of the market supply curve for broccoli
    d.   all of the above
    e.   none of the above

2.   In the previous question, if a university report indicates that broccoli contains important, hitherto-unrecognized ingredients that can help stave off cancer (which in fact happened in 1992),[1] the result is likely to be:

    a.   a shift to the right in the market supply curve for broccoli
    b.   a shift to the left in the market supply curve for broccoli
    c.   a shift to the right in the market demand curve for broccoli
    d.   all of the above
    e.   none of the above

3.   If the government reduces the subsidies to broccoli production, the equilibrium price of broccoli will:

    a.   fall
    b.   increase by $10
    c.   increase by $2
    d.   increase
    e.   be unaffected

4.   If the price of asparagus falls considerably, the result is likely to be:

    a.   a shift to the right in the market demand curve for broccoli
    b.   a shift to the left in the market supply curve for broccoli
    c.   a shift to the left in the market demand curve for broccoli
    d.   an increase in the equilibrium price of broccoli
    e.   none of the above

5.   If the price of asparagus falls considerably and the government freezes the price of broccoli at the level prevailing before the fall in the price of asparagus, the result is likely to be:

    a.   a surplus of broccoli
    b.   a shortage of broccoli
    c.   a shift to the left in the market supply curve for broccoli
    d.   a shift to the right in the market supply curve for broccoli
    e.   none of the above

Problems

1.   Based on unofficial estimates by economists at the U.S. Department of Agriculture, the market demand curve for wheat in the American market in the early 1960s was (roughly) as follows:

---

[1] *The New York Times*, March 25, 1992, p. C1.

Farm price of wheat (dollars per bushel)	Quantity of wheat demanded (millions of bushels)
1.00	1,500
1.20	1,300
1.40	1,100
1.60	900
1.80	800
2.00	700

In the middle 1970s, the market demand and supply curves for wheat in the American market were (roughly) as follows:

Farm price of wheat (dollars per bushel)	Quantity of wheat demanded (millions of bushels)	Quantity of wheat supplied (millions of bushels)
3.00	1,850	1,600
3.50	1,750	1,750
4.00	1,650	1,900
5.00	1,500	2,200

a. If the market demand curve in the middle 1970s had remained as it was in the early 1960s, can you tell whether the farm price of wheat in the middle 1970s would have been greater or less than $2? Explain.

b. Did a shift occur between the early 1960s and the middle 1970s in the market demand curve for wheat? If so, was it a shift to the right or the left, and what factors may have been responsible for this shift?

c. Suppose that the government had supported the price of wheat at $4 in the middle 1970s. How big would have been the excess supply? What would have been some of the objections to such a policy?

2. Assume that the quarterly demand and supply functions for personal computers (PCs) are

$$Q_D = 340 - 6P$$
$$Q_S = 100 + 2P$$

where price is in $100 of 2001 dollars, and quantity is in thousands of units.

a. What is the equilibrium price for PCs?

b. Assume that the United States found that foreign producers "dumped" PCs on the U.S. market and imposed a price floor of $3,250. Would this result in an excess supply of or demand for PCs, and how large would it be?

Answers

Wool: An Opening Example

a. Yes, because at each price more wool would be supplied than before.

b. Yes, because at each price less wool would be demanded than before.

    c. To compensate for the decrease in demand from the Chinese and Russians that, all else being equal, would have led to a decrease in price.

    d. When the Australian Wool Corporation no longer propped up the price, demand fell, yielding a lower equilibrium price.

True or False

    1. False   2. False   3. False   4. False   5. False

Multiple Choice

    1. b   2. c   3. d   4. c   5. a

Problems

1. a. It is impossible to tell. At \$2, the quantity demanded would have been 700 million bushels, but we are not given the quantity supplied at \$2. If it were greater than 700 million bushels, the equilibrium price would have been less than \$2; if it were less than 700 million bushels, the equilibrium price would have been greater than \$2.

    b. Yes. At \$3, the quantity of wheat demanded during the 1960s would have been less than 700 million bushels, if the demand curve was downward-sloping to the right. During the 1970s, 1,850 million bushels were demanded at \$3. Thus the demand curve seemed to shift to the right. This may have been due to increased foreign demand because of poor harvests in the Soviet Union, Australia, and Argentina, as well as devaluation of the dollar.

    c. 250 million bushels. Such surpluses have been an embarrassment, both economically and politically. They suggest that society's scarce resources are being utilized to produce products that consumers do not want at existing prices. Also, the cost of storing these surpluses can be large.

2. a. In equilibrium, $Q_D = Q_S$, so

$$340 - 6P = 100 + 2P$$
$$240 = 8P$$
$$P = 30$$

The equilibrium price is \$3,000 per PC.

    b. This would lead to excess supply (the price floor is above the equilibrium price) equal to

$$Q_E = 100 + 2(30) = 160$$
$$Q_S = 100 + 2(32.5) = 165$$
$$5,000 \text{ units}$$

Part Two
THE NATURE OF MARKETS

CHAPTER 2

Demand Theory

Chapter Profile

The **market demand curve** for a product shows how much will be sold at each price. The market demand curve shifts in response to changes in tastes, incomes, and the prices of other goods, as well as a host of other factors. **Demand** is a key determinant of a firm's profitability. Consequently, successful managers devote significant resources to analyzing the market and the demand for their product.

The **market demand function** for a product is an equation showing how the quantity demanded depends on the good's price, the incomes of consumers, the prices of other goods, advertising expenditure, and other factors. Holding all factors other than the product's price constant, one can derive the market demand curve for the product from the market demand function.

The **price elasticity of demand** is the percentage change in quantity demanded resulting from a very small change in price. The price elasticity measures whether a price increase (or decrease) results in an increase (decrease) in the total amount spent by consumers on a product.

Marginal revenue (*MR*) is the incremental change in total revenue (*TR*) resulting from selling an additional unit of a product.

$$MR = P\left[1 + \frac{1}{\eta}\right]$$

where P is price, and η is the price elasticity of demand.

The **price elasticity of demand** for a good tends to be high if it has a large number of close substitutes. Substitutes are other products in the marketplace that can be purchased to do approximately the same thing. Price elasticity also tends to be higher in the long run than in the short run. It is sometimes asserted that the demand for a product is relatively price inelastic if the product accounts for a very small percentage of the typical consumer's budget, but this need not be the case.

The **income elasticity of demand** is the percentage change in quantity demanded resulting from a very small increase in consumer income. The income elasticity of demand may be positive or negative. Like the price elasticity of demand, it is of major importance in forecasting the long-term growth of the quantity demanded for many major products.

The **cross elasticity of demand** is the percentage change in the quantity demanded of product *X* resulting from a 1 percent increase in the price of product *Y*. If *X* and *Y* are substitutes, it is positive; if they are complements, it is negative. (Complements are products that are usually purchased together, such as hamburgers and ketchup.) This elasticity is important to managers because they must try to understand and forecast the effects of changes in other firms' prices on their own firm's sales.

Key Formulas to Remember

1. Market demand function:

$$Q = b_1P + b_2I + b_3S + b_4A$$

where Q = quantity demanded, P = price, I = per-capita income level, S = price of a related product, and A = amount spent on advertising.

2. Price elasticity of demand:

$$\eta = \left[\frac{P}{Q}\right]\frac{\Delta Q}{\Delta P}$$

3. Cross elasticity of demand:

$$\eta = \left[\frac{P_y}{Q_x}\right]\frac{\Delta Q_x}{\Delta P_y}$$

where x and y are different products, and $\eta = \left[\frac{P}{Q}\right]\frac{dQ}{dP}$.

4. The relationship of marginal revenue to total revenue and elasticity (the example that follows is for a linear demand function):

$$P = a - bQ$$

The demand function is written here as normally graphed in economics, with price, P, on the y (dependent variable) axis, even though price is actually the independent variable.

$$TR = P \times Q = aQ + bQ^2$$

Marginal revenue is the change in revenue from the purchase of one additional unit (or, in calculus, the first derivative of TR), which is

$$MR = a + 2bQ$$

Note that the slope of the MR curve is twice that of the demand curve.

$$MR = P\left[1 + \frac{1}{\eta}\right], \quad MC = P\left[1 + \frac{1}{\eta}\right], \quad P = MC\left[\frac{1}{1 + 1/\eta}\right]$$

$$\eta_i = \left[\frac{dQ}{dP}\right]\left[\frac{I}{Q}\right], \quad \eta_{XY} = \left[\frac{dQ_X}{dP_Y}\right]\left[\frac{P_Y}{Q_X}\right]$$

Questions

Completion

1. If the cross elasticity of demand between goods X and Y is positive, these goods are classified as _____.

2. The income elasticity of demand is the percentage change in quantity demanded resulting from a(n) _____ change in money income.

3. Luxury goods are generally assumed to have a(n) _____ income elasticity of demand.

4. If a commodity has many close substitutes, its demand is likely to be _____.

5. The price elasticity of demand equals _____.

6. An increase in the price of a good that is a complement in consumption will _____ demand.

7. The price elasticity of demand is generally _____ in the long run than in the short run (for nondurable goods).

8. The total amount of money spent by consumers on a commodity equals the industry's _____.

9. The _____ curve shows marginal revenue at various quantities of output.

10. For normal goods, an increase in income will lead to a(n) _____ in demand.

True or False

_____ 1. The demand for open-heart surgery is likely to be less price elastic than the demand for aspirin.

_____ 2. If a good's income elasticity exceeds 1, a decrease in the price of the good will increase the total amount spent on it.

_____ 3. If a firm is on a portion of its demand curve that is price inelastic, it cannot be maximizing profits.

_____ 4. Under a linear demand function, as price increases, the price elasticity of demand becomes less elastic.

_____ 5. The demand for salt and pepper is likely to be price elastic.

_____ 6. In general, demand is likely to be more inelastic in the long run than in the short run (for nondurable goods).

_____ 7. The income elasticity of demand for food is very high.

_____ 8. It is always true that $\eta_{xy} = \eta_{yx}$.

_____ 9. The direct approach of simply asking people how much they would buy of a particular commodity is the best way to estimate the demand curve.

_____   10.   The income elasticity of demand will always have the same sign regardless of the level of income at which it is measured.

_____   11.   Marginal revenue is the ratio of the value of sales to the amount sold.

_____   12.   When the demand curve is linear, the slope of the marginal revenue curve is twice (in absolute value) the slope of the demand curve.

Multiple Choice

1. The president of a leading producer of tantalum says that an increase in the price of tantalum would have no effect on the total amount spent on tantalum. If this is true, the price elasticity of demand for tantalum is:

   a.   greater than zero
   b.   −1
   c.   −2
   d.   less than −1
   e.   none of the above

2. The demand for a good is price inelastic if:

   a.   the price elasticity is −1
   b.   the price elasticity is less than −1
   c.   the price elasticity is greater than −1
   d.   all of the above
   e.   none of the above

3. The relationship between marginal revenue and the price elasticity of demand is:

   a. $MR = P\left[1 + \dfrac{1}{\eta}\right]$

   b. $P = MR\left[1 + \dfrac{1}{\eta}\right]$

   c. $P = MR(1 - \eta)$
   d. $MR = P(1 - \eta)$
   e.   none of the above

4. A demand curve with unitary elasticity at all points is:

   a.   a straight line
   b.   a parabola
   c.   a hyperbola
   d.   all of the above
   e.   none of the above

5. Suppose we are concerned with the relationship between the quantity of food demanded and aggregate income. It seems most likely that this relationship will look like:

   a.   curve *A* below
   b.   curve *B* below
   c.   curve *C* below

d.   the vertical axis
e.   the horizontal axis

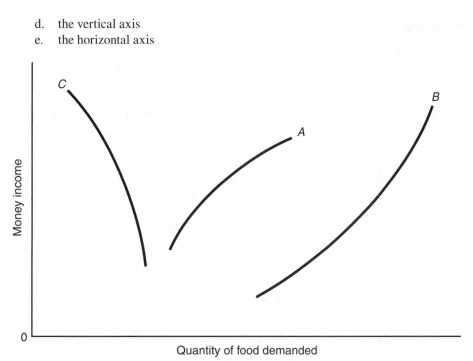

6.   If goods X and Y are substitutes, the relationship between the quantity demanded of good X and the price of good Y should be like:

a.   curve A below
b.   curve B below
c.   the vertical axis
d.   the horizontal axis
e.   none of the above

Problems

1. The Economic Research Service of the U.S. Department of Agriculture has reported the results of a study of the effects of the price of various types of oranges on the rate at which they were purchased.[2] In particular, three types of oranges were studied: (1) Florida Indian River, (2) Florida Interior, and (3) California. In nine test stores in Grand Rapids, Michigan, the researchers varied the price of each of these types of oranges for a month. The effect of a 1 percent increase in the price of each type of orange on the rate of purchase of this and each of the other types of oranges follows. For example, a 1 percent increase in the price of Florida Indian River oranges (holding other prices constant) seemed to result in a 3.1 percent decrease in the rate of purchase of Florida Indian River oranges, a 1.6 percent increase in the rate of purchase of Florida Interior oranges, and a 0.01 increase in the rate of purchase of California oranges.

	Results in the following percentage change in the rate of purchase of:		
A 1 percent increase in the price of:	*Florida Indian River*	*Florida Interior*	*California*
Florida Indian River	23.1	11.6	10.01
Florida Interior	11.2	23.0	10.1
California	10.2	10.1	22.8

    a. What seems to be the price elasticity of demand for each type of orange?
    b. What seems to be the cross elasticity of demand for each pair of types of oranges?
    c. Which types of oranges seem to be the closest substitutes?
    d. Of what use might these results be to orange producers?
    e. How accurate do you think this study was? What improvements would you make in it?

2. The price elasticity of demand for a particular kind of screwdriver is −2, and marginal revenue is $2. What is the profit-maximizing price of this screwdriver?

3. The president of your firm claims that the price elasticity of demand is the same as the slope of the demand curve. You (quite correctly) argue that this is not true. To buttress your point, you draw a linear demand curve (from *B* to *A* on the following grid) and point out that, although the slope is the same at all points along the demand curve, the price elasticity of demand differs from point to point. (Thus, the slope and the price elasticity of demand cannot be the same.) The president of your firm asks you to identify those points (on the demand curve you have drawn) where the demand for the product is price elastic, those points where it is price inelastic, and those points where it is of unitary elasticity. Respond to his request.

---

[2]M. Godwin, W. Chapman, and W. Manley, *Competition between Florida and California Valencia Oranges in the Fresh Market* (U.S. Department of Agriculture, December 1965). This paper is also summarized in G. Stokes, *Managerial Economics: A Casebook* (New York: Random House, 1969). The numbers have been changed slightly.

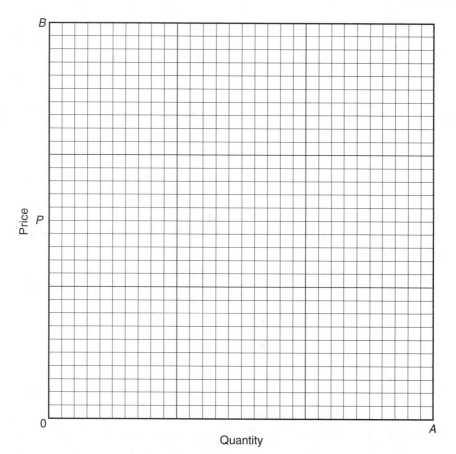

4. a. According to the president of Bethlehem Steel, the demand for steel is price inelastic because steel generally constitutes a very small percentage of the total cost of the product that includes it as a raw material. If this is the case, will a price increase result in an increase or decrease in the amount of money spent on steel?

 b. Suppose you are a business consultant and you become convinced that the U.S. steel industry underestimates the price elasticity of demand for steel. In what way might this information be useful to the steel companies? To the public?

5. a. According to Gregory Chow of Princeton University, the price elasticity of demand for automobiles in the United States is −1.2, and the income elasticity of demand for automobiles is 3. What would be the effect of a 3 percent decline in auto prices on the quantity of autos demanded, assuming Chow's estimates are right?

 b. What would be the effect of a 2 percent increase in income?

6. a. According to the Swedish economist Herman Wold's estimates, the income elasticity of demand for liquor is about 1. If you were an executive for a liquor firm, of what use might this fact be to you in forecasting sales?

b.   According to Rex Daly of the U.S. Department of Agriculture, the price elasticity of demand for coffee is about -0.25 to -0.30, and the income elasticity of demand is about 0.23. Suppose you were an economist for the coffee industry. How could you use this information to help forecast coffee sales in the United States?

7.   The Rosenberg Corporation, a maker of machine tools, determines that the demand curve for its product is as follows:

$$P = 1,000 - 50Q$$

where P is the price (in dollars) of a machine tool, and Q is the number of machine tools sold per month.

a.   What is the price elasticity of demand if price equals $400?
b.   At what price, if any, will the demand for Rosenberg's product be of unitary elasticity?

8.   The David Company's demand curve for the company's product is

$$P = 2,000 - 20Q$$

where P is the price, and Q is the number sold per month.

a.   Derive the marginal revenue curve for the firm.
b.   At what outputs is the demand for the firm's product price elastic?
c.   If the firm wants to maximize its dollar sales volume, what price should it charge?

9.   The Byron Company's marketing vice president concludes that the demand function for its product is

$$Q = 50P^{-1.3}I^{0.9}A^{0.2}$$

where Q is the quantity demanded per month, P is the product's price (in dollars), I is disposable income (in dollars), and A is the firm's advertising expenditures (in thousands of dollars).

a.   What is the price elasticity of demand?
b.   Will increases in price result in increases or decreases in the amount spent on Byron's product?
c.   What is the income elasticity of demand?
d.   What is the advertising elasticity of demand?

10.   The Keats Corporation estimates that its demand function is as follows:

$$Q = 200 - 2P + 3I + 0.5A$$

where Q is the quantity demanded per month, P is the product's price (in dollars), I is per-capita disposable income (in thousands of dollars), and A is the firm's advertising expenditures (in thousands of dollars per month). (In all parts of this problem, population is assumed to remain constant.)

a.   During the next decade, per-capita disposable income is expected to increase by about $3,000. What effect will this have on the firm's sales?
b.   If Keats wants to raise its price enough to offset the effect of the increase in per-capita disposable income, by how much must it raise its price?

c.   If Keats raises its price by this amount, will it increase or decrease the price elasticity of demand? Explain.

11. The president of the Malibu Corporation estimates that the demand function for the firm's product is

$$Q = 30P^{-2.5}I^{0.8}$$

where Q is the quantity demanded, P is the product's price, and I is disposable income. The marginal cost of the firm's product is estimated to be $40.

a.   Malibu's price for its product is $60. Is this the optimal price? Why or why not?

b.   If it is NOT the optimal price, write a brief memorandum indicating what price might be better, and why.

12. Harnischfeger, a leading machinery producer, tried to make major changes in the rough-terrain crane industry. It redesigned its cranes for easy manufacture and service through the use of modularized components and reduced material content. It established a conveyorized assembly line and ordered parts in large volumes. The firm's strategy was to become a low-cost producer in the industry. Based on its cost reductions, the firm was able to offer a product of acceptable quality and cut price by 15 percent, the result being that its market share increased from 15 to 25 percent.[3] Did the demand for its product seem to be price elastic? Explain. (Assume that the total quantity demanded in the market was the same before and after this price cut.)

Answers

Completion
1. substitutes   2. 1 percent   3. high   4. price elastic   5. $-\dfrac{\Delta Q_d}{\Delta P} \cdot \dfrac{P}{Q_D}\left[\dfrac{P}{Q_d}\right]\dfrac{\Delta Q_d}{\Delta P}$

6. decrease   7. higher   8. total revenue   9. marginal revenue   10. increase

True or False
1. True   2. False   3. False   4. False   5. False   6. False   7. False   8. False
9. False   10. False   11. False   12. True

Multiple Choice
1. b   2. b   3. a   4. c   5. b   6. b

Problems
1. a.   The price elasticity of demand for Florida Indian River oranges seems to be −3.1, the price elasticity of demand for Florida Interior oranges seems to be −3.0, and the price elasticity of demand for California oranges seems to be −2.8.

b.   The cross elasticities (η_{xy}) are as follows:

---

[3]M. Porter, *Competitive Strategy* (New York: Free Press, 1980), p. 37.

Y	Florida Indian River	X Florida Interior	California
Florida Indian River	—	1.6	0.01
Florida Interior	1.2	—	0.1
California	0.2	0.1	—

c. Clearly, Florida Indian River and Florida Interior oranges are closer substitutes than the Florida and California oranges.

d. The fact presented in part c is of obvious use to orange growers in both parts of the country.

e. The study is limited, of course, by the fact that it pertains to only one city during only one relatively short period of time.

2. Since $MR = P\left[1 + \dfrac{1}{\eta}\right]$, it follows that $P = MR \div \left[1 + \dfrac{1}{\eta}\right]$. In this case, $MR = \$2$ and $\eta = -2$; thus $P = \$2 \div \left[1 + \dfrac{1}{2}\right]$, or \$4. (MR = marginal revenue, P = price, and η = the price elasticity of demand.)

3. The demand curve you have drawn is BA.

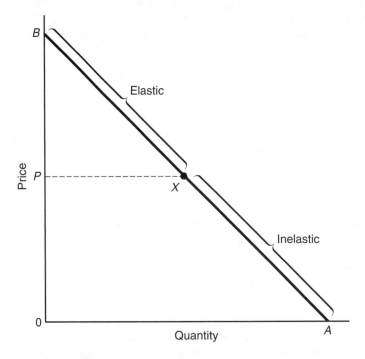

Point X is midway between points B and A.

4. a. It will result in an increase in the amount of money spent on steel.

b. It might indicate that both the companies and the public might be better off if steel prices were lowered somewhat, since the quantity demanded might expand more than heretofore expected.

5. a. There would be about a 3.6 percent increase in quantity demanded.
   b. There would be about a 6 percent increase in quantity demanded.

6. a. All other things equal, you could expect that a 1 percent increase in income would result in about a 1 percent increase in the total quantity of liquor demanded.
   b. A 1 percent change in price would be expected to result in about a 0.28 percent change in quantity demanded. A 1 percent increase in income would be expected to increase the quantity demanded by about 0.23 percent.

7. a. Since $P = 1,000 - 50Q$, it follows that $Q = 20 - 0.02P$. It follows that

$$\eta = \left[\frac{-0.02(400)}{12} \right]; \text{ that is, } \eta = -0.75.$$

   b. The price elasticity of demand equals one when the marginal revenue is equal to zero. Given that $MR = 1,000 - 100Q$, it follows that this is satisfied when $Q = 10$. This implies that price elasticity equals 1 when price equals $500.

8. a. $MR = 2,000 - 40Q$
   b. If the demand is price elastic, marginal revenue is positive. Thus, the demand is price elastic if

$$MR = 2,000 - 40Q > 0$$

   which is true if $Q < 50$.
   c. To maximize its dollar sales volume, the firm should set $dTR/dQ = 0$, where TR equals total revenue. Since dTR/dQ equals marginal revenue, this means that it should set marginal revenue equal to zero. Since $MR = 0$ when $Q = 50$, it follows that the price should be set at $1,000.

9. a. -1.3
   b. decreases
   c. 0.9
   d. 0.2

10. a. It will increase the quantity demanded per month by about 9.
    b. $4.50
    c. It will increase it.

11. a. To maximize profit, price should equal

$$\$40 \left[\frac{1}{1 - 1/2.5} \right]$$

   since the price elasticity of demand equals -2.5. Thus, price should be $40 \div 0.6 = \$66.67$.
   b. See part a.

12. Yes. Let Q be the total quantity demanded in the market (which we assume to be constant), and let P be the original price charged by the firm. The arc price elasticity of demand equals

$$-\left[\frac{0.25Q - 0.15Q}{0.20Q}\right] \div \left[\frac{0.85P - P}{0.925P}\right] = -3.1$$

13. Demand curve: $P = a + bQ$

Total revenue $= P \bullet Q = aQ + bQ^2$

Marginal revenue $\dfrac{\Delta TR}{\Delta Q} = a + 2bQ = \dfrac{dTR}{dQ} = a + 2bQ$

CHAPTER 3

Consumer Behavior and Rational Choice

Chapter Profile

An **indifference curve** contains points representing market baskets from which the consumer gets equal satisfaction. If the consumer prefers more (not less) of both commodities, an indifference curve must have a negative slope. Market baskets on higher indifference curves provide more satisfaction than those on lower indifference curves. Utility is a number that indexes the level of satisfaction derived from a particular market basket. Market baskets with higher utilities are preferred over market baskets with lower utilities. The marginal rate of substitution shows how many units of one good must be given up if the consumer, after getting an extra unit of another good, is to maintain a constant level of satisfaction. To obtain the marginal rate of substitution, multiply the slope of the indifference curve by -1.

The **budget line** contains all of the market baskets that the consumer can buy, given his or her money income and the level of each price. Increases in income push the budget line upward; changes in the price ratio alter the budget line's slope. To attain the highest level of satisfaction that is compatible with the budget line, the consumer must choose the market basket on the budget line that is on the highest indifference curve. This market basket is at a point where the budget line is tangent to an indifference curve (unless there is a corner solution). A consumer who maximizes utility will choose in equilibrium to allocate his or her income so that the marginal rate of substitution of one good for another good equals the ratio of the prices of the two goods (unless there is a corner solution).

The theory of consumer behavior is often used to represent the process of rational choice. Frequently, a person or an organization has a certain amount of money to spend and must decide how much to allocate to a number of different uses. This theory indicates how such decisions should be made.

A consumer's **demand curve** shows how much the consumer will purchase of the good in question at various prices of the good, when other prices and the consumer's income are held constant. The theory of consumer behavior can be used to derive the consumer's demand curve, and the market demand curve can be obtained by summing the individual demand curves horizontally.

Clearly, many consumers are willing to pay more than the market price for a commodity. This is evident from the downward shape of the demand function. The difference between what consumers are willing and able to pay for a commodity and the price they do pay is referred to as **consumer surplus**. When aggregated over consumers, it is the area between the horizontal line centered on the equilibrium market price and the demand curve.

Key Formulas to Remember

1. Marginal rate of substitution:

$$MRS = -\frac{X_b}{X_a}$$

where two goods, *a* and *b*, are on the *Y* and *X* axes, respectively. The *MRS* shows how much of one good you are willing to give up for another good (this ratio changes as one moves along the indifference curve).

2. The budget line:

$$I = YP_a + XP_b \text{ and solving for } Y, Y = \frac{I}{P_b} - \frac{P_b}{P_a}X$$

where *I* = income, P_a and P_b are the prices of goods *a* and *b*, and therefore, the slope

of the budget line is $-\frac{P_b}{P_a}$. And the point where the slope of the budget line is equal

to the *MRS* (the ratio of what you are willing to substitute of one good for the other) represents the most that you can get of both goods, given your income level.

Questions

Completion

1. All other things being equal, it is assumed that the consumer always prefers _____ of a commodity to _____ of a commodity.

2. Economists assume that the consumer attempts to _____ utility.

3. The consumer, when confronted with two alternative _____, can decide which he or she prefers or whether he or she is _____ between them.

4. If one market basket has more of one commodity than a second market basket, it must have (less, more) _____ of the other commodity than the second market basket—assuming that the two market baskets are to yield equal _____ to the consumer.

5. Besides knowing the consumer's preferences, we must also know his or her _____ and the _____ of commodities to predict which market basket he or she will buy.

6. Every indifference curve must slope (downward, upward) _____ and to the right to reflect the fact that commodities are defined so that (less, more) _____ of them are preferred to (less, more) _____.

7. Since market baskets on higher indifference curves are given (higher, lower) _____ utilities, and since market baskets on higher indifference curves are always (preferred, not preferred) _____ to market baskets on lower indifference curves, the consumer will always choose a market basket with a

(higher, lower) _____ utility over a market basket with a (higher, lower) _____ utility.

8. The consumer's _____ shows what he or she wants, and the consumer's _____ shows which market baskets his or her income and prices permit him or her to buy.

9. An increase in money income means that the budget line (falls, rises) _____, and a decrease in money income means that the budget line (falls, rises) _____.

10. Commodity prices affect the budget line: A decrease in a commodity's price causes the budget line to cut this commodity's axis at a point (closer to, farther from) _____ the origin.

True or False

_____ 1. If the consumer's tastes were transitive, the consumer would have inconsistent or contradictory preferences.

_____ 2. According to the theory of consumer behavior, the consumer's equilibrium market basket is the one that yields maximum utility, given the constraints imposed on the consumer by his or her income and by prices.

_____ 3. The best way to allocate the military budget is to spend it all on the highest priority item of each service.

_____ 4. A utility is a number that represents the level of satisfaction the consumer derives from a particular market basket.

_____ 5. Indifference curves cannot intersect.

_____ 6. Market baskets on higher indifference curves must have lower utilities than market baskets on lower indifference curves.

_____ 7. The consumer's budget line shows the market baskets that can be purchased, given the consumer's income and prevailing commodity prices.

_____ 8. The higher is the consumer's money income, the lower the budget line.

_____ 9. A consumer buys two goods: U and V. If the price of a unit of U is equal to the price of a unit of V, the slope of the consumer's budget line is -1.

_____ 10. Two consumers buy two goods: U and V. The first consumer is located in a region where the price of U is higher than in the region where the second consumer is located. The price of V is the same in both regions. Nonetheless, if the first consumer's income is higher than the second consumer's, it is possible for the two consumers' budget lines to be parallel.

Multiple Choice

1. An increase in the consumer's income will:

   a. shift the budget line outward from the origin but not affect its slope
   b. shift the budget line outward from the origin and increase its slope

    c.   shift the budget line outward from the origin and decrease its slope
    d.   not shift the budget line
    e.   none of the above

2.   In equilibrium, the rate at which the consumer is willing to substitute one commodity for another (holding satisfaction constant) must equal:

    a.   the consumer's income
    b.   the price of the good on the horizontal axis
    c.   the price of the good on the vertical axis
    d.   the rate at which the consumer is able to substitute one good for the other
    e.   none of the above

3.   The marginal rate of substitution is:

    a.   the slope of the consumer's indifference curve
    b.   the slope of the consumer's indifference curve multiplied by −1
    c.   always equal to the price ratio
    d.   never equal to the price ratio
    e.   none of the above

4.   Indifference curves can intersect if:

    a.   the consumer is poorly educated
    b.   the two goods are high priced
    c.   the consumer's income is very low
    d.   all of the above
    e.   none of the above

5.   If the expected return from an investment is plotted along the vertical axis and the riskiness of the investment is plotted along the horizontal axis, the indifference curve of the investor will be positively sloped if:

    a.   the investor does not care what rate of return he or she receives
    b.   the investor does not care how risky an investment is
    c.   the investor prefers a more risky to a less risky investment, when the expected rate of return is held constant.
    d.   all of the above
    e.   none of the above

Problems

1.   Suppose Sandy gets the same utility from each of the six combinations of goods Z and W that follow. Good Z costs $10 per unit, and good W costs $4 per unit.

Commodity combination

	1	2	3	4	5	6
Amount of good W *(units)*	1	2	4	7	11	16
Amount of good Z *(units)*	10	9	8	7	6	5

    a.   What is the minimum income she must have to achieve the level of utility associated with these commodity combinations?
    b.   If she has the income you found in part a, draw her budget line.

c. Draw her indifference curve.

2. Draw the indifference curve that includes the following market baskets in the following graph. Each of these market baskets gives the consumer equal satisfaction.

Market basket	Meat (pounds)	Potatoes (pounds)
A	1	9
B	2	8
C	3	7
D	4	6
E	5	5
F	6	4
G	7	3
H	8	2

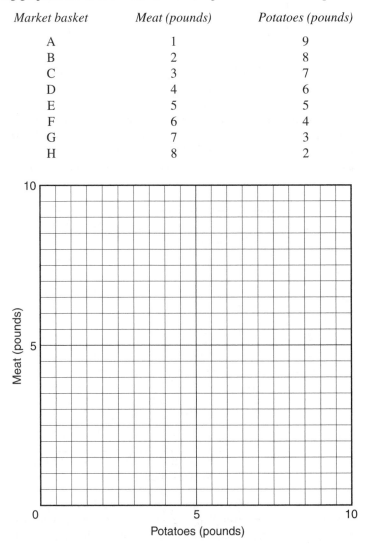

3. a. Suppose that the consumer has an income of $10 per period and must spend it all on meat or potatoes. If meat is $1 a pound and potatoes are 10 cents a pound, draw the consumer's budget line.

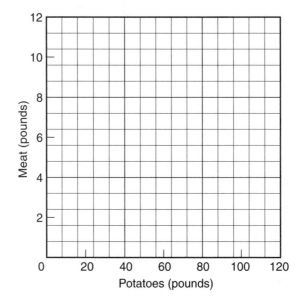

    b. What will be the budget line if the consumer's income increases to $12? What will be the budget line if the consumer's income is $10, but the price of meat increases to $2 per pound? What will be the budget line if the consumer's income is $10, and the price of meat is $1 per pound, but the price of potatoes increases to 20 cents per pound?

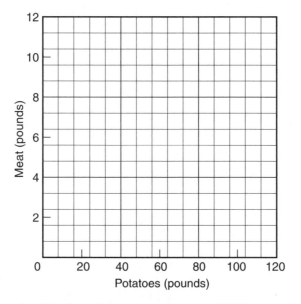

4. a. Suppose that John Jones has a money income of $100 per week, and he spends it all on nails and fertilizer. Suppose fertilizer is $2.50 per pound and nails are $1.00 per pound. Draw John Jones's budget line on the graph that follows:

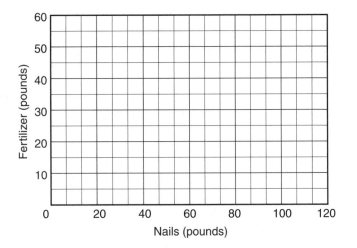

b. Suppose that John Jones has the following set of indifference curves:

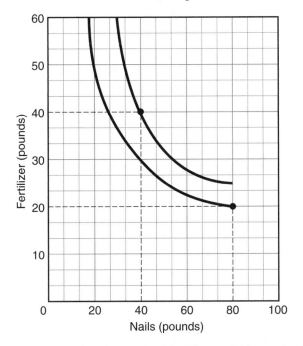

Does John Jones prefer 40 pounds of fertilizer and 40 pounds of nails to 20 pounds of fertilizer and 80 pounds of nails? Why or why not?

c. Suppose that John Jones's money income is $100 per week and that fertilizer is $1.67 per pound and nails are $1.25 per pound. Based on the information in part b, what (approximately) is his equilibrium market basket?

5. Sally spends all her income of $3,000 per month on two goods, X and Z, whose prices are $30 and $60, respectively. She is currently spending half her income on each good and is maximizing her utility.

a. How much of each good is she consuming?
b. Represent Sally's utility-maximizing consumption of each good, given her tastes, income, and the price of each good in the following graph.

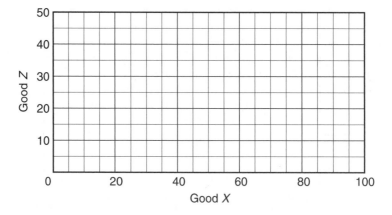

c. Draw her budget line in the graph.
d. Using your diagram, show that, if she is now offered a choice of 10 additional units of good X for free or $300 extra income, she cannot be worse off, and may be better off, by taking the $300. Explain why this is true.

6. The straight lines that follow are budget lines. The curved lines are indifference curves of Mr. William White. The budget lines assume that Mr. White's income is $500 per week.

a. What is the price of a piece of clothing? Explain your reasoning.
b. Specify two points on Mr. White's demand curve for food.

Answers

Completion

1. more, less   2. maximize   3. market baskets, indifferent   4. less, satisfaction
5. income, prices   6. downward, more, less   7. higher, preferred, higher, lower
8. indifference curve, budget line   9. rises, falls   10. farther from

True or False

1. False 2. True 3. False 4. True 5. True 6. False 7. True 8. False
9. True 10. False

Multiple Choice

1. a 2. d 3. b 4. e 5. e

Problems

1. a. $96
   b. and c.

2.

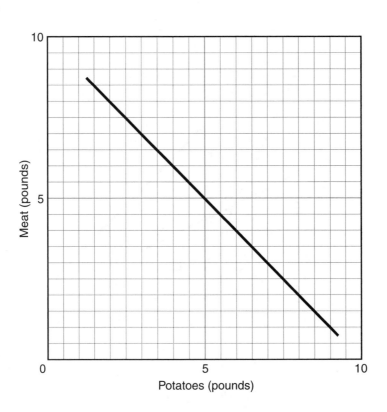

3. a. The consumer's budget line follows.

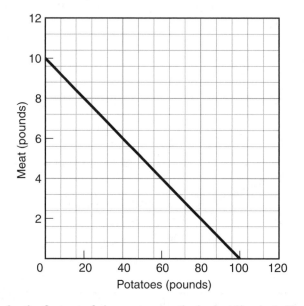

b. Under the first set of circumstances, the budget line is *A*. Under the second set of circumstances, it is *B*. And under the third set of circumstances, it is *C*.

4. a.

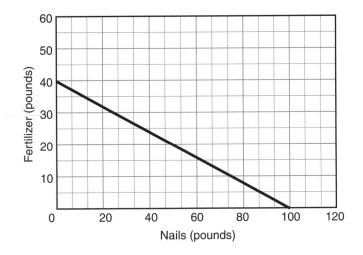

    b. Yes. Because it is on the higher indifference curve.
    c. It is difficult to tell from the diagram exactly what the equilibrium market basket will be, but it will contain about 25 to 40 pounds of nails and about 30 to 40 pounds of fertilizer.

5. a. Quantity of $X = 50$, quantity of $Z = 25$.
    b. and c.

    d. If the $300 in income was allocated to good X, she could purchase 10 more units. Given that the cash provides her with the option of either making this purchase or reallocating to another market basket, she cannot be worse off with the cash.

6. a. The price must be $100 per piece since the budget line (which pertains to an income of $500) intersects the horizontal axis at 5 pieces.
    b. At $10 per pound, he consumes 30 pounds of food. At $5 per pound he consumes 40 pounds of food.

CASE ONE

How H-P Used Tactics of the Japanese to Beat Them at Their Game
Stephen Kreider Yoder

It was such sweet revenge.

Last year, Hewlett-Packard Co. faced a challenge from NEC Corp. The Japanese giant had plans to attack H-P's hegemony in the burgeoning computer-printer market in time-honored Japanese fashion: by undercutting prices with new, better-designed models. Over a decade ago, the tactic helped other Japanese companies grab the lead from H-P in a business it had pioneered, hand-held calculators.

This time it didn't work. Months before NEC could introduce its inexpensive monochrome inkjet printer, H-P launched an improved color version and slashed prices on its bestselling black-and-white model by 40% over six months. NEC withdrew its entry, now overpriced and uncompetitive, after about four months on the market.

"We were too late," says John McIntyre, then a marketing director at NEC's U.S. Unit. "We just didn't have the economies of scale" to compete with H-P.

A few years ago, U.S. companies were ruing Japan's unbeatable speed to market and economies of scale in many industries, and printers were a prime example: Japan made four out of five personal-computer printers that Americans bought in 1985.

But now many American and Japanese companies are trading places, a shift confirmed by an annual global survey that reported Tuesday that the U.S. has replaced Japan as the world's most competitive economy for the first time since 1985.

H-P is one of the most dramatic of an increasing number of U.S. take-back stories, in technologies including disk drives, cellular phones, pagers and computer chips. H-P didn't even start making PC printers until 1984, but it is expected to have about $8 billion in printer revenue this year.

H-P's Dominance
Hewlett-Packard's U.S. printer market share

Source: Dataquest

Stephen Yoder, "How H-P Used Tactics of the Japanese to Beat Them at Their Game," from *The Wall Street Journal*.

Among other things, the H-P story dispels common myths about the relative strengths of the U.S. and Japan, showing how big U.S. companies, under proper leadership, can exploit American creativity while using their huge resources to deploy "Japanese" tactics. H-P used its financial might to invest heavily in a laboratory breakthrough, then kept market share by enforcing rules that are gospel in Japan: Go for mass markets, cut costs, sustain a rapid fire of product variations and price cuts, and target the enemy.

Richard Hackborn, the H-P executive who led the charge, also succeeded because he could do what his Japanese counterparts couldn't: Buck the system. His printer-business teams were in outposts like Boise, Idaho—far from H-P's increasingly bureaucratic Palo Alto, Calif., headquarters—where they were permitted, though sometimes reluctantly, to go their own way.

H-P's other top executives for the most part preached high-profit, high-cost products for niche markets—which is how H-P lost the calculator business. Mr. Hackborn's troops set profit margins below the corporate norm and went for the mass market themselves. They moved fast and defied corporate rules when it meant winning customers.

"If you're going to leverage American culture but compete globally, you need a balance of entrepreneurship and central leverage," says Mr. Hackborn, who retired last year to become an H-P director. "The rugged individualism of cowboy culture alone doesn't work; but to be centrally directed doesn't either, because you lose the tremendous contribution of local innovation and accountability."

Japanese industrialists have often sermonized about U.S. complacency and myopia, but Japanese success, it turns out, can breed the same. H-P kept its huge lead because Japanese manufacturers, flush with success, spent too long squeezing profits out of old technologies and ignored signs that the American market—the bellwether— was rapidly changing.

"H-P understood computers better, it understood American customers better, it got good products to market faster," says Takashi Saito, head of Canon Inc.'s inkjet-printer business. Japanese makers' culture hindered the kind of quick decision-making needed in the fast-paced U.S. computer market, he says, and as a result, "The market is H-P's garden."

Hewlett-Packard's journey to the top of the printer market began with a laboratory accident in 1979 and culminated in a rout of the Japanese beginning in 1992.

When H-P started thinking of entering the printer market, it realized it couldn't unseat the dominant Japanese makers, such as Seiko Epson Corp. and Oki Electric Industry Co., without a technological advance. Japan had a lock on the mass market with low-cost, well-engineered "dot matrix" printers, which form relatively rough letters.

The seeds for the H-P breakthrough had been nurtured by engineers in a converted janitor's closet at a Vancouver, Wash., plant since 1980. The year before, an H-P scientist noticed drops of liquid splattered over his lab bench. He had been testing a thin metal film by zapping it with electricity; when the metal grew hot, liquid trapped underneath began to boil and spurted out. The discovery evolved into the "thermal" inkjet.

Mr. Hackborn saw that inkjet technology had compelling advantages over laser printers for the mass market: It was cheaper, it was more easily adaptable for color printing and no one else had perfected it. The idea of using a jet to spit ink on paper had been around for years, but no one had found a good way to pump the ink through tiny holes.

H-P's first inkjet printer in 1984 was hardly a knockout. It needed special paper, the ink tended to smear and it could print only 96 dots per inch, compared with today's 600 dots. "H-P's first inkjet was terrible quality," says Norio Niwa, president of Epson's U.S. unit. "Our engineers thought that if they announced such a product, they'd lose face."

H-P saw it differently. It had also introduced a successful line of expensive laser printers for corporate customers, but the company believed that ordinary computer users would soon demand higher-quality printouts of text, graphics and photographs. There was a mass market in the making—the kind that H-P had previously blown. To prevent a repeat, H-P had to invest heavily in its low-cost inkjet technology, Mr. Hackborn says, and "learn from the Japanese" by building it into a family of products.

Meanwhile, the Japanese were making mistakes. Canon, which had edged ahead of H-P in patenting early inkjet designs but had agreed to share the patents, chose a complex implementation that would set it years behind. And Epson, the king of dot-matrix printers, ignored warnings of changing consumer tastes.

Executives from Epson's U.S. unit began traveling to Japan around 1985 to tell headquarters that low-budget PC users would soon demand high-quality printers and that Epson should invest more in technologies such as inkjets, says Peter Bergman, a former Epson marketing executive. "Their approach was, 'Who are these Americans to come over and tell me how to build our products?'" he says.

Epson had an inkjet technology of its own, but it was an expensive variation. Besides, says Mr. Niwa, the Epson executive, "Every engineer was looking at dot matrix because we had a big market, big profits, big business, and the technology itself had a long history."

The same kind of mistake could have happened at H-P. Headquarters became increasingly bureaucratic, with product plans requiring many levels of approval. But business units are set up as fiefs, each

having great autonomy. "We had the resources of a big company, but we were off on our own," says Richard Belluzzo, who has taken over from Mr. Hackborn. "There wasn't central planning..., so we could make decisions really fast."

A PATENT OFFENSE

Based on decisions made in the hinterlands, H-P engineers adopted two Japanese tactics: They filed a blizzard of patents to protect their design and frustrate rivals, and embarked on a process of continual improvement to solve the inkjet's problems. They developed print heads that could spit 300 dots an inch and made inks that would stay liquid in the cartridge but dry instantly on plain paper. One engineer tested all types of paper: bonded, construction, toilet—and, for good measure, added sandpaper, tortillas and socks.

In 1988, H-P introduced the Deskjet, the plain-paper printer that would evolve into the model now taking market share away from the Japanese. No rivals loomed, but the line still wasn't meeting sales goals in 1989. It was competing with H-P's own more costly laser printers. Sales were too low to pay the high costs of research and factories. The inkjet division needed new markets to avert a financial crisis.

That autumn, a group of engineers and managers assembled for a two-day retreat at a lodge on Oregon's Mount Hood. They pored over market-share charts. That, says Richard Snyder, who now heads H-P's PC inkjet business, is "when the lights went on." H-P hadn't targeted the right enemy. Instead of positioning the inkjet as a low-cost alternative to H-P's fancy laser printers, the managers decided, they should go after the Japanese-dominated dot-matrix market.

Dot matrix, the biggest section of the market, had serious flaws—poor print quality and color. Epson, the No. 1 player, had a soft underbelly: No competitive inkjet and the distraction of an expensive and failing effort to sell a PC. "We said, 'Maybe this is a good time to attack,'" Mr. Snyder says.

H-P did so with the obsessive efficiency of a Japanese company. A week later, H-P teams were wearing "Beat Epson" football jerseys. The company began tracking Epson's market share, studying its marketing practices and public financial data, surveying loyal Epson customers and compiling profiles of Epson's top managers. Engineers tore apart Epson printers for ideas on design and manufacturing, a tactic the Japanese often use.

Among the findings: Epson's marketers got stores to put their printers in the most prominent spots; Epson used price cuts as tactical weapons to fend off challengers; consumers like Epson machines for their reliability; Epson's printers were built to be manufactured easily. H-P responded, demanding that stores put its inkjet printers alongside Epson's. It tripled its warranty to three years and redesigned printers with manufacturing in mind.

Engineers learned Epson got huge mileage out of a product by creating a broad line consisting of slight variations of the same basic printer. By contrast, "we were taken with the notion at H-P that you had to come up with a whole new platform every time," Mr. Snyder says. Change came hard. In 1990, as H-P was developing a color printer, engineers were set on creating a completely new, full-featured mechanical marvel. Marketers suggested that a simpler, slightly clumsier approach, would be good enough for most consumers.

TWEAKING A "KLUDGE"

There was a near mutiny among the engineers until a product manager named Judy Thorpe forced them to do telephone polls of customers. It turned out people were eager for the product the engineers considered a "kludge." H-P learned that "you can tweak your not-so-latest thing and get the latest thing," Ms. Thorpe says. By sticking to the existing platform, H-P was able to get the jump on competitors in the now-booming color-printer market.

By 1992, it became clear to Japanese makers that dot-matrix printers were under assault, with sales falling for the first time as inkjet sales soared.

When the Computer City division of Tandy Corp., the Fort Worth, Texas, company, was preparing to open its first stores in the summer of 1991, it told printer makers that it expected inkjets to be a hot category, says Alan Bush, president of the chain. The Japanese responded that they didn't have anything ready. "We were very astounded," says Mr. Bush. "In the summer of '91, for an inkjet-product line you had your choice: H-P, H-P or H-P."

When Japanese printer makers that had been investing in inkjet research tried to move into the market, they ran into a brick wall: H-P had a lock on many important patents. Citizen Watch Co. found H-P had "covered the bases to make it very difficult for anyone else to get there," says Michael Del Vecchio, senior vice president of Citizen's U.S. unit. Citizen engineers trying to develop print heads learned H-P had some 50 patents covering how ink travels through the head. "It's like being in a maze: You go down this path and suddenly you're into an area that may infringe on their main patents and you have to back up and start over."

This barrier to entry meant competitors lost valuable time. "Every year that went by that we and other people were unsuccessful in reinventing the wheel, [H-P] got a greater and greater lead," says Mr. McIntyre, the former NEC executive.

Then there were H-P's economies of scale, which allowed it to undercut almost anyone else's prices; by the time Canon came out with the first credible competition, H-P had sold millions of printers and had thousands of outlets for its replacement cartridges. And H-P used its experience to make continual improvements in manufacturing. In constant dollars, for example, today's Deskjet costs half as much to make as the 1988 model.

This has allowed H-P to carry out a vital strategy: When a rival attacks, hit back quickly and hard. When Canon was about to introduce a color inkjet printer last year, H-P cut the price of its own version before its rival had even reached the market. The black-and-white printer, priced at $995 in 1988, now lists for $365.

Inkjets Take Over
North American printer shipments, in millions of units
Source: Dataquest   *Projection

"They've been very good about eating their own young," Mr. McIntyre says.

And consuming the competition as well. H-P now holds 55% of the world market for inkjets. The success in printers, including lasers, has propelled enormous overall growth at H-P, making it one of the two fastest-growing major U.S. multinationals (the other is Motorola Inc.). H-P's other divisions have been transformed by the printer people's mass-market approach and now seek to make the lowest-cost personal and hand-held computers on the market.

H-P's lead in printers could bring even more profits because inkjet mechanisms are finding their way into facsimile machines and color copiers. Sales could explode if, as expected, inkjet becomes the technology of choice inside TV-top printers for interactive-TV services. Printers will "be like toilets," says Mr. Hackborn. "They'll play a central role in the home."

Questions

1. Before introducing its inkjet printers, did Hewlett-Packard have to estimate the demand curve for them? Why or why not?

2. When studying Epson before going after the Japanese-dominated dot-matrix market, did Hewlett-Packard try to determine which factors would have an important influence on the demand curve for its product? If so, what factors seemed to be particularly important?

3. Hewlett-Packard cut the price of its black-and-white printer from $995 to $365. If the quantity of such printers that it sold per year increased tenfold, does this mean that the (arc) price elasticity of demand for this product was about 1.8? Why or why not?

4. Can the data in the graph on page 35 be used to determine the trend in Hewlett-Packard's printer market share? What are the limitations of these data for such purposes?

5. If you were hired by Hewlett-Packard to forecast how many inkjet printers it would sell next year, how would you go about doing it? What data would you need? What techniques would you use? How accurate do you think your forecast would be?

Part Three
PRODUCTION AND COST

CHAPTER 4

Production Theory

Chapter Profile

The **production function** precisely specifies the relationship between the quantities of various inputs used and the quantity of the products that can be produced in any given time period. Given the production function for a particular firm, one can calculate the **average product** of an input (total output divided by the amount of the input) and the **marginal product** of an input (the addition to total output resulting from the addition of the last unit of input, when the amounts of other inputs used are held constant).

To determine how much of a particular input to utilize, a firm should compare the marginal revenue product of the input (the amount that an additional unit of the input adds to total revenue) with the marginal expenditure on the input (the amount that an additional unit of the input adds to total cost). To maximize profit, the firm should utilize the amount of the input that results in the marginal revenue product being equal to the marginal expenditure.

An **isoquant** is a curve showing all possible (efficient) combinations of inputs that are capable of producing a particular quantity of output. The marginal rate of technical substitution shows the rate at which one input can be substituted for another input if output remains constant. No profit-maximizing firm will operate at a point where the isoquant is positively sloped (that is, where it takes more of all inputs to produce the same quantity of output).

An **isocost curve** shows all of the input bundles that can be purchased for a specific expenditure of money. To minimize the cost of producing a particular output, a firm should allocate the expenditures among various inputs in such a way that the ratio of the marginal product to the price is the same for all inputs used. Graphically, this amounts to choosing the input combination where the relevant isoquant is tangent to an isocost curve.

The **law of diminishing marginal returns** is a well-known occurrence where equal increments of a particular input (such as more workers) are added while holding all other input levels the same. The incremental increases to output (**marginal product**) eventually get smaller and may even lessen output.

If the firm increases all inputs by the same proportion and output increases by more (less) than this proportion, there are **increasing (decreasing) returns to scale**. Increasing returns to scale may occur because of indivisibility of inputs, various geometrical relations, or specialization. Decreasing returns to scale can also occur; the most frequently cited reason is the difficulty of managing a huge enterprise. Whether or not there are constant, increasing, or decreasing returns to scale is an empirical question that must be settled case by case. Note that increasing (decreasing) returns to scale should not be confused with increasing (decreasing) costs with scale, as described in Chapter 5 and often referred to as "economies of scale."

Managers commonly use the **Cobb-Douglas production function** for estimating a production function. This formulation had the advantage of having the marginal productivity of each input depend on the level of all inputs employed which is often in business a realistic assumption.

Key Formulas to Remember

1. Production function:

$$Q = f(X_1, X_2, \ldots, X)$$

and the marginal product $MP_{X1} = \dfrac{\Delta Q}{\Delta X_1} \cdot \dfrac{\Delta Q}{\Delta X_2}$ $MP_{X1} = \dfrac{\Delta Q}{\Delta X_1}, \dfrac{\Delta Q}{\Delta X_2}$ and so forth.

2. Marginal rate of technical substitution:

$$MRTS = -\dfrac{\Delta X_2}{\Delta X_1} = \dfrac{MP_1}{MP_2} \quad MRTS = -\dfrac{dX_2}{dX_1} = -\dfrac{MP_1}{MP_2}$$

3. Total outlays:

$$M = P_L + P_K$$

where L = labor and K = capital (assume two inputs only); and

$$K = \dfrac{M}{P_K} - \dfrac{P_L L}{P_K}$$

Therefore, the slope of the isocost curve $= -\dfrac{P_L}{P_K}$.

4. And, therefore, you would produce at the output where

$$-\dfrac{P_L}{P_K} = -\dfrac{MP_K}{MP_L} \text{ or } \dfrac{MP_K}{P_K} = \dfrac{MP_L}{P_L}$$

the point where the ratio of the MP to the P of all inputs is the same.

5. Cobb-Douglas production function:

$$Q = aL^b K^c$$

Questions

Completion

1. At the Manchester Corporation, the average product of labor equals $3L$, where L is the number of units of labor employed per day. The total output produced per day if 4 units of labor are employed per day is _____. The total output produced

per day if 5 units of labor are employed per day is _____. The marginal product of the fifth unit of labor employed per day is _____.

2. In the _____, all inputs are variable.

3. The _____ production function can be written $Q = AL^{\alpha_1} K^{\alpha_2}$.

4. A fixed input is _____.

5. A variable input is _____.

6. In both the short run and the long run, a firm's productive processes generally permit substantial _____ in the proportions in which inputs are used.

7. The average product of an input is total product divided by _____.

8. The marginal product of an input is the addition to total output resulting from

_____.

9. Underlying the law of diminishing marginal returns is the assumption that technology remains _____.

10. Two isoquants can never _____.

True or False

_____   1. If the average product of labor equals 10/L, where L is the number of units of labor employed per day, total output is the same regardless of how much labor is used per day.

_____   2. The law of diminishing marginal returns is inconsistent with increasing returns to scale.

_____   3. The marginal rate of technical substitution equals −1 times the slope of the isoquant.

_____   4. Isoquants are always straight lines.

_____   5. All production functions exhibit constant returns to scale.

_____   6. Increasing returns to scale can occur because of the difficulty of coordinating a large enterprise.

_____   7. Whether there are increasing, decreasing, or constant returns to scale in a particular case is an empirical question.

_____   8. Statistical studies of production functions are hampered by the fact that available data do not always represent technically efficient combinations of inputs and outputs.

_____   9. The production function is not closely related to a firm's or industry's technology.

_____   10. The law of diminishing marginal returns applies to cases where there is a proportional increase in all inputs.

Multiple Choice

1. At the Martin Company, the average product of labor equals $5/L^{0.5}$, where L is the amount of labor employed per day. Thus:

   a. labor always is subject to diminishing marginal returns
   b. labor is subject to diminishing marginal returns only when L is greater than 5
   c. labor always is not subject to diminishing marginal returns
   d. labor always is not subject to diminishing marginal returns when L is greater than 5
   e. none of the above

2. Suppose that the production function is as follows:

Quantity of output per year	Quantity of input per year
2	1
5	2
9	3
12	4
14	5
15	6
15	7
14	8

   The average product of the input when 7 units of the input are used is:

   a. 7
   b. 15
   c. 15/7
   d. 7/15
   e. none of the above

3. If the production function is as given in question 2, the marginal product of the input when between 1 and 2 units of the input is used is:

   a. 2
   b. 5
   c. 3
   d. 4
   e. none of the above

4. If the production function is as given in question 2, the marginal product of the input begins to decline:

   a. after 3 units of input are used
   b. after 2 units of input are used
   c. after 4 units of input are used
   d. after 7 units of input are used
   e. none of the above

5. If the production function is as given in question 2, the marginal product of the input is negative when more than:

 a. 7 units of input are used
 b. 6 units of input are used
 c. 5 units of input are used
 d. 4 units of input are used
 e. none of the above

6. The marginal product equals the average product when the latter is:

 a. 1/2 of its maximum value
 b. 1/4 of its maximum value
 c. equal to its maximum value
 d. 1 1/2 times its maximum value
 e. none of the above

7. Given $Q = 10\,K^{0.5}L^{0.4}$, where K represents the units of capital and L the hours of labor employed in production, which of the following is a true statement regarding the marginal product of labor?

 a. It is smaller than the marginal product of capital.
 b. It is decreasing with respect to capital.
 c. It is increasing with respect to labor.
 d. It satisfies the property of diminishing marginal returns.
 e. none of the above

8. If the production function is the same as is given in question 7, which of the following is a true statement regarding the marginal product of capital?

 a. It is smaller than the marginal product of labor.
 b. It is decreasing with respect to labor.
 c. It is increasing with respect to capital.
 d. It satisfies the property of diminishing marginal returns.
 e. none of the above

9. If the production function is the same as is given in question 7, which of the following statements is true?

 a. It is consistent with increasing returns to scale.
 b. It is consistent with constant returns to scale.
 c. It is consistent with decreasing returns to scale.
 d. It is inconsistent with the law of diminishing marginal returns.
 e. both c and d

10. If the production function is the same as is given in question 7 and the inputs were doubled, output would:

 a. double
 b. increase by 190 percent
 c. increase by 90 percent
 d. remain unchanged
 e. none of the above

Problems

1. a. Suppose the production function for a cigarette factory is as follows, there being only one input:

Amount of input *(units per year)*	*Amount of output* *(units per year)*
1	7
2	14.5
3	22
4	29
5	35
6	39
7	39

Plot the average product curve for the input in the following graph.

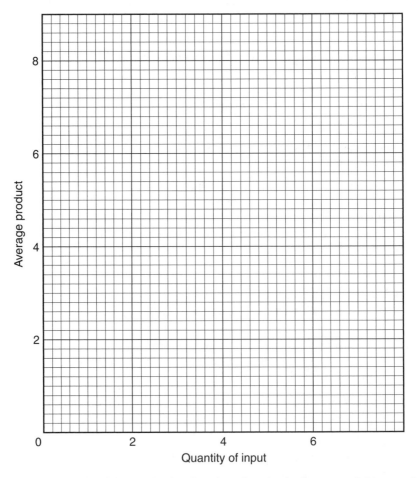

b. On the basis of the production function given in the first part of this question, plot the marginal product curve of the input.

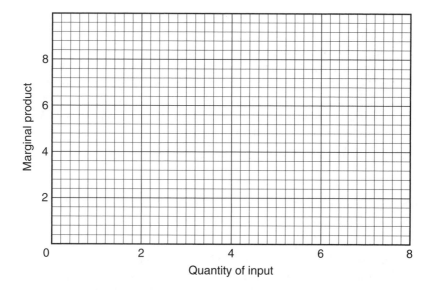

2. a.   In the Cobb-Douglas production function, is the exponent of labor generally larger or smaller than that of capital?
   b.   Suppose that in a chemical plant $Q = aL^\alpha K^\beta$, where Q is the output rate, L is the rate of labor input, and K is the rate of capital input. Statistical analysis indicates that $\alpha = 0.8$ and $\beta = 0.3$. The owner of the plant claims that there are increasing returns to scale in the plant. Is he right?
   c.   What is the value of the output elasticity in the firm in part b?

3. If the owner of a firm with the following production function, $Q = 5K^{0.7}L^{0.5}$, states that the firm should decrease the scale of operations in order to increase the economic efficiency of production, is she correct? Why?

4. The Concord Company produces 20,000 parts of a particular type per year. The cost of each setup is $5,000, and the annual cost of holding each identical part of this sort in inventory for a year is $2. What is the optimal lot size?

5. In industries like consumer electronics, steel, and autos, the Japanese have increased their share of the American market. An engineering comparison of a compact-car plant in Japan and the United States is as follows:

	United States	*Japan*
Parts stamped per hour	325	550
Personnel per press line	7–13	1
Time needed to change dies	4–6 hours	5 minutes
Average production run	10 days	2 days
Time needed per small car	59.9 hours	30.8 hours
Number of quality inspectors	1 per 7 workers	1 per 30 workers

   a.   One of the concepts at the core of Japanese production management is "just-in-time" production, which calls for goods being produced and delivered just in time to be sold, subassemblies to be produced and delivered just in time to be assembled into finished goods, and fabricated parts to be produced and delivered just in time to go into subassemblies. What are the advantages of this system?

b. What are the disadvantages of this system?

c. Another major Japanese production concept is "total quality control," or "quality at the source," which means that errors should be found and corrected *by the people performing the work*. In the West, inspection has often been performed by statistical sampling *after* a lot of goods is produced. What are the advantages of the Japanese system?

6. The production function for the Roundtree Laser Company is

$$Q = 10L^{0.5}K^{0.3}M^{0.3}$$

where Q is the number of lasers produced per week, L is the amount of labor used per week, K is the amount of capital used per week, and M is the quantity of raw materials used per week.

a. Does this production function exhibit diminishing marginal returns?

b. Does this production function exhibit decreasing returns to scale?

c. Does the average product of labor depend on the amount of the other inputs used?

7. At the Oklahoma Piano Company, the average product of labor equals 5, regardless of how much labor is used.

a. What is the marginal product of the first unit of labor?

b. What is the marginal product of the eightieth unit of labor?

c. By how much will output increase if labor is increased by 100 units?

d. By how much will output fall if labor is reduced by 50 units?

e. Does this case conform to the law of diminishing marginal returns? Why or why not?

f. Does this case seem realistic? Why or why not?

8. The Torch Corporation, a hypothetical producer of paper napkins, claims that in 2001 it has the following production function:

$$Q = 3 + 4L + 2P$$

where Q is the number of paper napkins it produces per year, L is the number of hours of labor per year, and P is the number of pounds of paper used per year.

a. Does this production function seem to include all of the relevant inputs? Explain.

b. Does this production function seem reasonable if it is applied to all possible values of L and P? Explain.

c. Does this production function exhibit diminishing marginal returns?

9. Fill in the blanks in the following table:

Number of unit of variable input	Total output (number of units)	Marginal product* of variable input	Average product of variable input
3	——	Unknown	30
4	——	20	——
5	130	——	——
6	——	5	——
7	——	——	19½

*These figures pertain to the interval between the indicated amount of the variable input and one unit less than the indicated amount of the variable input.

10. As the quantity of a variable input increases, explain why the point where marginal product begins to decline is encountered before the point where average product begins to decline. Explain too why the point where average product begins to decline is encountered before the point where total product begins to decline.

11. The Deering Company's production function is $Q = 20LK$, where Q is the output rate, L is the number of units of labor it uses per period of time, and K is the number of units of capital it uses per period of time. The price of labor is $4 a unit, and the price of capital is $10 per unit. What combination of inputs should the firm use to produce 200 units of output per period of time?

12. The Barton Company is a manufacturer of spectrometers. Barton's vice president for operations has determined that the firm's output (Q) is related in the following way to the number of engineers used (E) and the number of technicians used (T):

$$Q = -5.682 - 0.316E - 0.417T + 6.3512(E)^{0.5} + 8.5155\ (T)^{0.5} + 0.3410(ET)^{0.5}$$

Suppose the wage of an engineer is $36,000, the wage of a technician is $24,000, and the total amount that the firm spends on both engineers and technicians is limited to $6 million. Find two equations that must be satisfied simultaneously to obtain the optimal values of E and T.

13. The owner of the Martin Marina believes that the relationship between the number of boats serviced and labor input is

$$Q = -3 + 8.5L - 2L^2$$

where Q is the number of boats serviced per hour, and L is the number of people employed. Her firm receives $20 for each boat serviced, and the wage rate for each person employed is $10.

a. How many people should she employ to maximize profit?
b. What will be the firm's hourly profit? (Assume that the only cost is labor cost.)

Answers

Completion
1. 48, 75, 27   2. long run   3. Cobb-Douglas   4. fixed in quantity
5. variable in quantity   6. variation   7. the quantity of the input
8. an extra unit of the input   9. constant   10. intersect

True or False

1. True   2. False   3. True   4. False   5. False   6. False   7. True
8. True   9. False   10. False

Multiple Choice

1. a   2. c   3. c   4. a   5. a   6. c   7. d   8. d   9. c   10. c

Problems

1. a.   The average product curve is as follows:

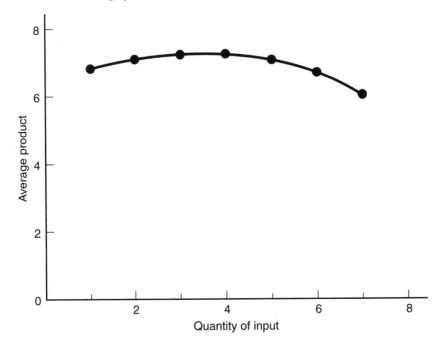

b.   The marginal product curve is as follows:

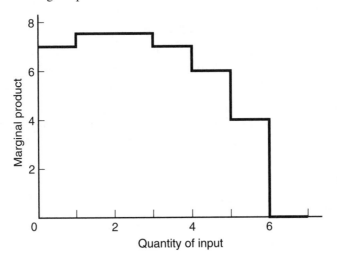

2. a. It is generally larger than the exponent of capital.
   b. Yes.
   c. 1.1

3. She is incorrect. The production function displays increasing returns to scale, implying that decreases in the scale of operations (level of inputs to production) will lead to a more than equal reduction in output. This implies less efficiency at a smaller scale.

4. The optimal lot size equals $\left[\dfrac{2(5,000)(20,000)}{2} \right]^{0.5} = 10,000.$

5. a. Because of its hand-to-mouth nature, just-in-time production means that a firm holds fewer inventories of parts, subassemblies, and finished goods. Because it is expensive to hold inventories, this is an advantage. Also, defects tend to be discovered more quickly, and their causes may be nipped in the bud.
   b. If goods, subassemblies, and parts are to be produced and delivered just in time for use or sale, they must be produced in small lots, which means that the equipment used to produce them must be set up more often. Each setup is expensive; it often involves moving heavy dies into place, making adjustments, and inspecting the results until the settings are right. To overcome this disadvantage, the Japanese have worked very hard to reduce setup costs. For example, Toyota has reduced the time to set up 800-ton presses used in forming auto hoods and fenders from an hour in 1971 to about 10 minutes or less.
   c. Higher quality of product, less waste of materials, a heightened awareness of the causes of defects on the part of the people doing the work, and fewer inspectors.

6. a. Yes.
   b. No.
   c. Yes.

7. a. 5
   b. 5
   c. 500
   d. 250
   e. No.
   f. No.

8. a. No. It seems likely that some capital and land are used.
   b. No. It says that an extra 1/4 hour of labor or an extra 1/2 pound of paper will result in an extra paper napkin, regardless of the number of paper napkins produced. Beyond some output level, one would expect the marginal product of labor and of paper to fall. Also, this seems to be a lot of labor and paper to produce one napkin!
   c. No.

9. The complete table is:

Number of units of variable input	Total output (number of units)	Marginal product of variable input	Average product of variable input
3	90	Unknown	30
4	110	20	27½
5	130	20	26
6	135	5	22½
7	136½	1½	19½

10. Because of the law of diminishing marginal returns, the marginal product begins to decline at some point. If the marginal product exceeds the average product at that point, the marginal product can fall to some extent without reducing the average product. Only when it falls below zero will the total product begin to decrease.

11. The firm wants to minimize

$$C = 4L + 10K$$

Since $K = 200 \div 20L = 10 \div L$, the firm wants to minimize

$$C = 4L + 10 \left[\frac{10}{L} \right]$$

Setting $dC/dL = 0$, we find that

$$\frac{dC}{dL} = 4 - \frac{100}{L^2} - 0$$

so $L = 5$. Thus, $K = 10 \div 5 = 2$. In other words, the firm should use 5 units of labor and 2 units of capital.

12. If the Barton Company is to maximize output, it must choose a combination of engineers and technicians such that

$$\frac{MP_E}{P_E} = \frac{MP_T}{P_T}$$

where MP_E is the marginal product of an engineer, MP_T is the marginal product of a technician, P_E is the wage of an engineer, and P_T is the wage of a technician. From the production function given in the question,

$$MP_E = \frac{\Delta Q}{\Delta E} = -0.316 + 3.1756 \left[\frac{1}{E} \right]^{-0.5} + 0.1705 \left[\frac{T}{E} \right]^{0.5}$$

$$MP_E = \frac{\partial Q}{\partial E} = -0.316 + 3.1756 \left[\frac{1}{E} \right]^{0.5} + 0.1705 \left[\frac{T}{E} \right]^{0.5}$$

$$MP_E = \frac{\Delta Q}{\Delta T} = -0.417 + 4.12578 \left[\frac{1}{T} \right]^{-0.5} + 0.1705 \left[\frac{E}{T} \right]^{0.5}$$

$$MP_T = \frac{\partial Q}{\partial T} = -0.417 + 4.12578 \left[\frac{1}{T} \right]^{0.5} + 0.1705 \left[\frac{E}{T} \right]^{0.5}$$

Substituting for MP_E and MP_T, and noting that $P_E = 36$ and $P_T = 24$ (since wages are measured in thousands of dollars), it follows that

$$\frac{1}{36}\left[-0.316 + 3.1756\left[\frac{1}{E}\right]^{0.5} + 0.1705\left[\frac{T}{E}\right]^{0.5}\right]$$

$$\frac{1}{24}\left[-0.417 + 4.2578\left[\frac{1}{T}\right]^{0.5} + 0.1705\left[\frac{E}{T}\right]^{0.5}\right]$$

Also, since the firm wants to spend only $6 million on engineers and technicians,

$$36E + 24T = 6{,}000$$

These last two equations must be solved simultaneously. (It turns out that the Barton Company should hire about 91 engineers and about 114 technicians.)

13. a. The marginal revenue product of a worker equals

$$20\frac{\Delta Q}{\Delta L} = 20(8.5 - 4L) = 170 - 80L \quad 20\left[\frac{dQ}{dL}\right]$$
$$= 20(8.5 - 4L) = 170 - 80L$$

Setting the marginal revenue product equal to the marginal expenditure on labor (which equals the wage), we find that

$$170 - 80L = 10$$

which means that $L = 2$. She should employ 2 people.
Hourly profit equals

$$20[-3 + 8.5(2) - 2(2)^2] - 2(10)$$
$$= 20(17 - 11) - 20 = 100$$

Thus, hourly profit equals $100.

CHAPTER 5

The Analysis of Costs

Chapter Profile

Managerial economists define the cost of producing a particular product as the value of the other products that the resources used in its production could have produced instead. This is called the product's opportunity cost, and another way of defining opportunity cost is the revenue forgone if resources (inputs) are not optimally used. It should be noted that the opportunity cost may differ from other cost numbers such as historical cost or replacement cost, which are used by firms for accounting or regulatory purposes.

In the short run, it is important to distinguish between a firm's **fixed** and **variable** costs. Fixed costs are those that cannot be changed in a given period of time (the short run). Variable costs, as the name implies, are within a manager's discretion to change at any time. The firm's total and average costs, total and average fixed costs, and total and average variable costs can all be plotted against output—as can the firm's marginal cost. The resulting **cost functions**, or cost curves (as they are often called), show how changes in output will affect the firm's costs, a major concern of any firm.

The long-run average cost function shows the minimum cost per unit of producing each output level when any desired scale of plant can be built. The long-run average cost curve is important for practical decision making because it shows the extent to which larger plants have cost advantages over smaller ones.

In choosing among plants, a major consideration is flexibility if the output of the plant is highly uncertain. Some plants, while they have higher costs than others at the most likely output, have lower costs than the others over a wide range of output. If one cannot predict output reasonably well, flexible plants of this sort may be best.

Break-even analysis compares total revenue and total cost, graphically or algebraically. A break-even chart combines the total cost function and the total revenue curve, both of which are generally assumed to be linear, and shows the profit or loss resulting from each sales level. The **break-even point** is the sales level that must be achieved if the firm is to avoid losses. Firms often find it useful to carry out various types of profit contribution analysis. The **profit contribution** is the difference between total revenue and total variable cost; on a per-unit basis, it is equal to price minus average variable cost.

Key Formulas to Remember

To combine the production function with the cost functions:

1. Average variable cost:

$$AVC = \frac{TVC}{Q} = W\left[\frac{U}{Q}\right] = W\left[\frac{1}{AVP}\right]$$

where W = wage rate (the cost of labor), U = the quantity of labor (number of employees), and Q = output.

2. Marginal cost:

$$MC = \frac{\Delta TVC + \Delta TFC}{\Delta Q} = \frac{\Delta TVC}{\Delta Q} = W\left[\frac{1}{MP}\right]$$

3. Economies of scope:

$$S = \frac{C(Q)_1 + C(Q)_2 - C(Q_1 + Q_1)}{C(Q_1 + Q_2)}$$

in other words, the ratio of the costs of producing two outputs separately minus the cost of producing them together divided by the costs of producing them together.

4. Break-even point:

$$Q_B = \frac{TFC}{P - AVC}$$

in other words, the output at which total revenue just equals total cost.

Questions

Completion

1. If the average fixed cost of producing 10 units of output at the Hollywood Manufacturing Company is $10, the average fixed cost of producing 20 units is _____. If the marginal cost of each of the first 20 units of output is $5, the average variable cost of producing 20 units is _____, and the average total cost of producing 20 units is _____.

2. Total cost equals _____ plus variable cost.

3. Average cost must equal marginal cost at the point where average cost is a(n) _____ .

4. The long-run total cost equals output times _____.

5. _____ include opportunity costs of resources owned and used by the firm's owner.

6. An important criticism of cross-section studies of cost functions is that they sometimes are subject to the _____.

7. Some determinants of the shape of the long-run average cost curve are

    _____.

8. The average variable-cost curve turns up beyond some output level because of the

    _____.

9. The marginal cost curve turns up beyond some output level because of the

    _____.

10. Average variable cost equals the price of the variable input divided by _____, if the price of the variable input is constant.

11. Marginal cost equals the price of the variable input divided by _____, if the price of the variable input is constant.

12. Statistical estimates of cost functions based on cross-section data sometimes run into problems because firms' _____ methods are different.

True or False

_____   1. If average variable cost always equals $20 when output is less than 100 units, marginal cost is less than $20 when output is in this range.

_____   2. Long-run marginal cost can never differ from short-run marginal cost.

_____   3. Costs that have already been incurred are important factors in making production decisions.

_____   4. The opportunity cost doctrine says that the production of one good may reduce the cost of another good.

_____   5. When the firm has constructed the scale of plant that is optimal for producing a given level of output, long-run marginal cost will equal short-run marginal cost at that output.

_____   6. The shape of the long-run average cost function is due primarily to the law of diminishing marginal returns.

_____   7. Average cost must exceed marginal cost at the point where average cost is a minimum.

_____   8. The break-even point lies well above the output level that must be reached if the firm is to avoid losses.

_____   9. Empirical studies often indicate that the short-run average cost curve is S-shaped.

_____   10. The survivor technique is a way of estimating a firm's short-run cost function.

Multiple Choice

1. The Moulton Corporation's average total cost per month equals $5 \times Q$, where Q is the number of units of output produced per month. The marginal cost of the third unit of output produced per month is:

    a. $15
    b. $20
    c. $25
    d. $30
    e. none of the above

2. The curve in the graph that follows has the shape of:

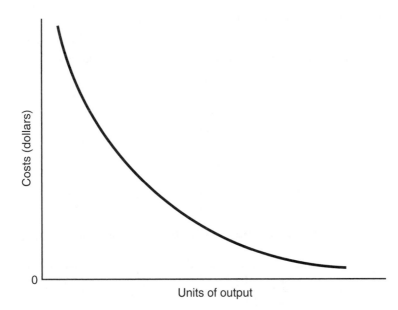

    a. a marginal cost curve
    b. an average variable-cost curve
    c. an average fixed cost curve
    d. all of the above
    e. none of the above

3. The firm's cost functions are determined by:

    a. the price of its product
    b. its assets
    c. its production function
    d. the age of the firm
    e. none of the above

4. A firm's marginal cost of production equals its average cost of production. Which of the following statements is therefore true?

    a. Marginal cost is at a minimum.
    b. Total cost is fixed.

    c.   Average cost is at a maximum.
    d.   Average cost is at a minimum.
    e.   none of the above

5. Decreasing long-run average costs are consistent with:

    a.   constant returns to scale
    b.   increasing returns to scale
    c.   diminishing marginal product
    d.   decreasing returns to scale
    e.   both b and c

Problems

1. Suppose that a machine shop's daily costs are as follows.

Units of output	Total fixed cost (dollars)	Total variable cost (dollars)
0	$500	0
1	500	50
2	500	90
3	500	140
4	500	200
5	500	270
6	500	350
7	500	450
8	500	600

    a.   Draw the firm's average fixed cost function in the following graph.

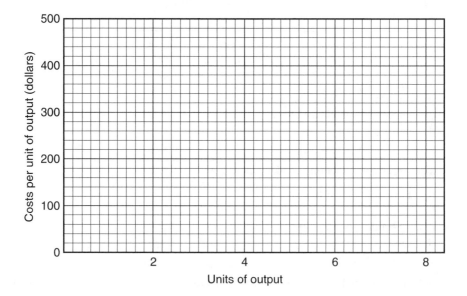

b. Draw the firm's average variable cost function.

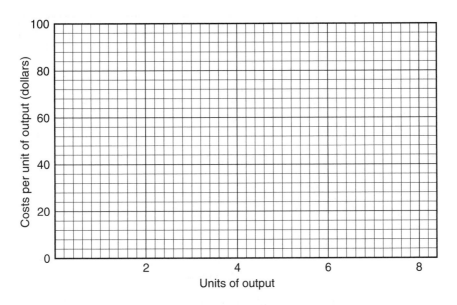

c. Draw the firm's average total cost function.

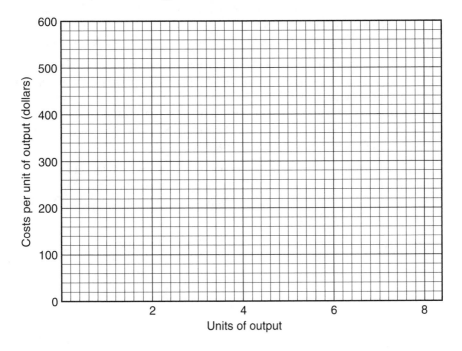

d. Draw the firm's marginal cost function.

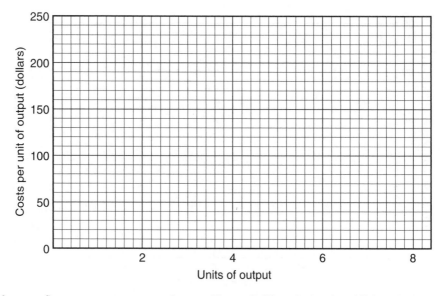

2. a. Suppose you are a consultant to HarperCollins, the book publisher. Suppose the firm is about to publish a book that will sell for $10 a copy. The fixed costs of publishing the books are $5,000; the variable cost is $5 a copy. What is the break-even point for this book?

b. If the price were $8 rather than $10, what would be the break-even point?

3. a. Suppose two firms have exactly the same marginal cost curve, but their average fixed cost curve is not the same. Will their average variable cost curve be the same? Why or why not?

b. A firm's marginal product of capital is twice its marginal product of labor; the price of labor is $6, and the price of capital is $3. Is the firm minimizing cost? If not, how can it reduce its costs? Explain.

4. Brady Farms is a profit-maximizing, perfectly competitive producer of tomatoes. It produces tomatoes using one acre of land (price of the land equals $2,000) and varying numbers of workers (wage per worker equals $500 per week). The production function is as follows:

Number of workers (per week)	Output of tomatoes (per week in truckloads)
0	0
1	1
3	2
7	3
12	4
18	5
25	6

Show that this farm is subject to increasing marginal cost as output increases.

5. The Miracle Manufacturing Company's short-run average cost function in 1999 is

$$AC = 3 + 4Q$$

where AC is the firm's average cost (in dollars per pound of the product) and Q is its output rate.

    a. Obtain an equation for the firm's short-run total cost function.
    b. Does the firm have any fixed costs? Explain.
    c. If the price of the Miracle Manufacturing Company's product (per pound) is $2, is the firm making profits or losses? Explain.

6. Show that a firm will maximize output—for a given outlay—by distributing its expenditures among various inputs in such a way that the marginal product of a dollar's worth of any input is equal to the marginal product of a dollar's worth of any other input that is used. At any point on a firm's cost function, is the firm maximizing output for a given outlay?

7. a. Suppose that capital and labor are the only inputs used by the Golden Printing Company and that capital costs $1 a unit and labor costs $2 a unit. Draw the isocost curves corresponding to an outlay of $200 and $300.

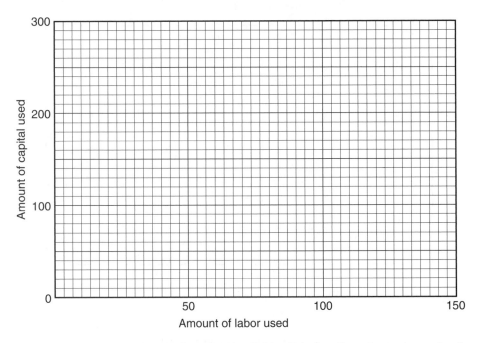

    b. To produce each unit of output, the Golden Printing Company must use 1 unit of labor and 1 unit of capital. What is the firm's cost of producing 200 units of output? Of producing 300 units of output?

8. The Barbizon Corporation is considering two types of plants to make an electric motor. For each type of plant, average variable cost is constant so long as output is

less than capacity, which is the maximum output of the plant. The cost structure for each type of plant is as follows:

	Plant X	Plant Y
Average variable costs		
Labor	$24.40	$12.10
Materials	14.10	14.05
Other	11.20	10.80
Total	$49.70	$36.95
Total fixed cost	$150,000	$400,000
Annual capacity	80,000	160,000

a. Derive the average cost of producing 40,000, 80,000, and 160,000 motors per year with plant X. (For outputs exceeding the capacity of a single plant, assume that more than one plant of this type is built.)

b. Derive the average cost of producing 40,000, 80,000, and 160,000 motors per year with plant Y.

c. If these are the only plants to produce these motors, plot the points on the long-run average cost curve for the production of these motors for outputs of 40,000, 80,000, and 160,000 per year.

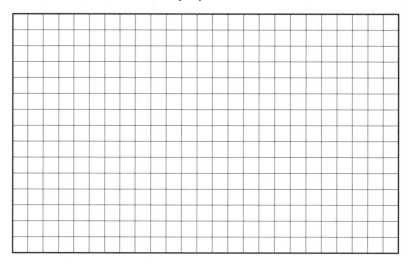

9. The Suffern Company's total cost function is

$$C = 100 + 3Q - 2Q^2 + 3Q^3$$

where C equals total cost and Q equals output per day.

a. What is the equation for the firm's average cost curve?

b. What is the equation for the firm's marginal cost curve?

c. At what output is marginal cost a minimum?

10. The Swarthmore Company is considering three types of plants to make a particular product. Plant I is much more highly automated than plant II, which in turn is more highly automated than plant III. For each type of plant, average variable cost is constant so long as output is less than capacity, which is the maximum output of the plant. The cost structure for each type of plant is as follows:

	Plant I	Plant II	Plant III
Average variable costs			
Labor	$1.60	$4.60	$5.80
Materials	1.10	1.50	1.90
Other	.60	.90	1.50
Total	$3.30	$7.00	$9.20
Total fixed costs	$600,000	$200,000	$100,000
Annual capacity (units)	200,000	100,000	50,000

   a. Derive the average cost of producing 200,000 units per year with plant I.
   b. Derive the average cost of producing 200,000 units per year with plant II. (For outputs exceeding the capacity of a single plant, assume that more than one plant of this type is built.)
   c. Derive the average cost of producing 200,000 units per year with plant III. (For outputs exceeding the capacity of a single plant, assume that more than one plant of this type is built.)

11. The Allentown Corporation, a retail seller of sofas, wants to determine how many sofas it must sell in order to earn a profit of $15,000 per month. The price of each sofa is $400, and the average variable cost is $150.

   a. What is the required sales volume if the Allentown Corporation's monthly fixed costs are $4,000 per month?
   b. If the firm sold each sofa at a price of $500, rather than $400, what would be the required sales volume?
   c. If the price is $500 and if average variable cost is $100, rather than $150, what would be the required sales volume?

12. According to a statistical study, the following relationship exists between a firm's total cost (TC) and its output (Q):

$$TC = 40 + 3Q + 2Q^2$$

At what output is average total cost a minimum?

13. Martin-Brower, a leading food distributor, pared its customer list to only eight fast-food chains. Its strategy was to satisfy the specialized needs of these customers at very low cost. To do so, it stocked only their narrow product lines, located its warehouses near their locations, and geared its order-taking procedures to their purchasing cycles. While Martin-Brower was not the lowest-cost distributor in serving the market as a whole, it was the lowest-cost in serving its particular part of the market, the result being that it was fast-growing and relatively profitable.[1] Is it always a good strategy for a firm to serve a highly specialized market?

---

[1]M. Porter, *Competitive Strategy* (New York: Free Press, 1980).

14. Complete the following table.

Output	TC	MC	AC
1	45	dna	———
2	———	9	———
3	67	———	———
4	———	21	———

Answers

Completion
1. $5, $5, $10   2. fixed cost   3. minimum   4. long-run average cost
5. Implicit costs   6. regression fallacy   7. economies and diseconomies of scale
8. law of diminishing marginal returns   9. law of diminishing marginal returns
10. average variable product   11. marginal product   12. accounting

True or False
1. False   2. False   3. False   4. False   5. True   6. False   7. False   8. False
9. False   10. False

Multiple Choice
1. c   2. c   3. c   4. d   5. e

Problems
1. a.

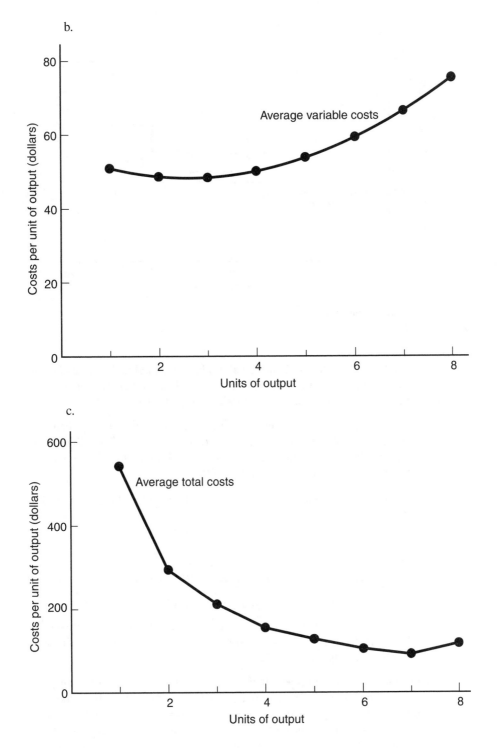

b.

Average variable costs

c.

Average total costs

d.

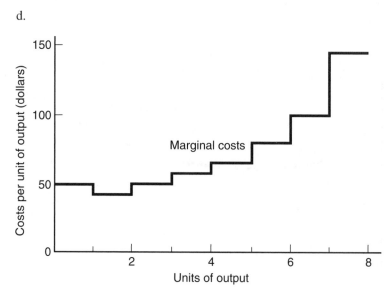

2. a. 1,000 copies sold.
   b. 1,667 copies sold.

3. a. Yes.
   b. No. Since the ratio of the marginal product of capital to the price of capital exceeds the ratio of the marginal product of labor to the price of labor, the firm can lower its costs by substituting capital for labor.

4. The *extra* labor needed to produce the first, second, third, fourth, fifth, and sixth truckloads of tomatoes are 1, 2, 4, 5, 6, and 7 workers. Thus, the marginal costs of the first, second, third, fourth, fifth, and sixth truckloads are $500, $1,000, $2,000, $2,500, $3,000, and $3,500.

5. a. Since total cost equals average cost times output, the firm's total cost function is

$$C = AC \cdot Q = 3Q + 4Q^2$$

   b. No, since total cost equals zero when $Q = 0$.
   c. If the price is $2, total revenue ($R$) equals $2Q$. Thus, the firm's profit equals

$$\pi = R - C = 2Q - (3Q + 4Q^2) = -Q - 4Q^2$$

   If Q is greater than zero, π must be negative, and the firm is incurring losses. If the firm is producing nothing, it is incurring neither profits nor losses. Thus, the firm is better off to produce nothing.

6. Draw the firm's isoquants as follows. Also draw the isocost curve corresponding to a given outlay. Clearly, point P is the input combination that maximizes output for this outlay. Since the firm's isoquant is tangent to the isocost curve at point P, the slope of the isocost curve (which equals $-1 \times$ the price of input $1 \div$ price of input 2) must equal the slope of the isoquant (which equals $-1 \times$ the marginal product of input $1 \div$ marginal product of input 2). Thus, at point P, the ratio of the marginal product to the price of each input must be the same. Yes.

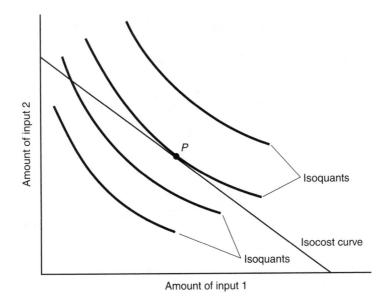

7. a. The isocost curves are as follows:

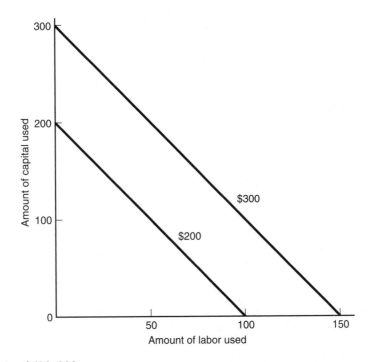

b. $600, 900

8. a. The average cost of producing 40,000 motors per year is
$49.70 + $\dfrac{$150,000}{40,000}$ = $49.70 + $3.75 = 53.45. For 80,000 and 160,000 motors, it is $49.70 + 1.88 = 51.58.

b. For 40,000 motors, it is $\$36.95 + \dfrac{\$400,000}{40,000} = \$46.95$. For 80,000 motors,

it is $\$36.95 + \dfrac{\$400,000}{80,000} = \$41.95$. For 160,000 motors, it is

$\$36.95 + \dfrac{\$400,000}{160,000} = \$39.45$.

c.

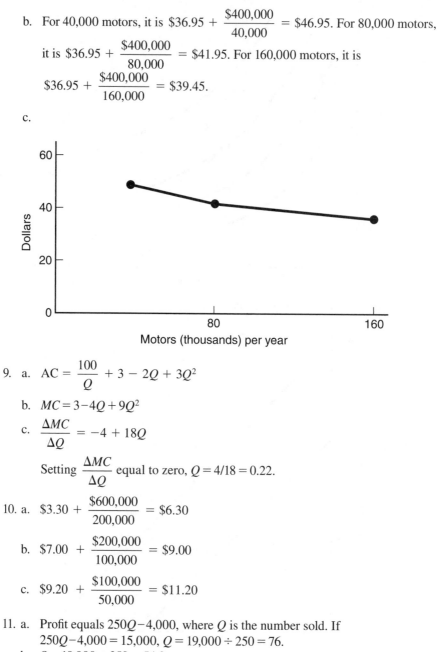

9. a. $AC = \dfrac{100}{Q} + 3 - 2Q + 3Q^2$

b. $MC = 3 - 4Q + 9Q^2$

c. $\dfrac{\Delta MC}{\Delta Q} = -4 + 18Q$

Setting $\dfrac{\Delta MC}{\Delta Q}$ equal to zero, $Q = 4/18 = 0.22$.

10. a. $\$3.30 + \dfrac{\$600,000}{200,000} = \$6.30$

b. $\$7.00 + \dfrac{\$200,000}{100,000} = \$9.00$

c. $\$9.20 + \dfrac{\$100,000}{50,000} = \$11.20$

11. a. Profit equals $250Q - 4,000$, where Q is the number sold. If
        $250Q - 4,000 = 15,000$, $Q = 19,000 \div 250 = 76$.
    b. $Q = 19,000 \div 350 = 54.3$
    c. $Q = 19,000 \div 400 = 47.5$

12. Average total cost equals

$$ATC = \dfrac{40}{Q} + 3 + 2Q$$

and

$$\frac{\Delta ATC}{\Delta Q} = \frac{-40}{Q^2} + 2$$

Setting $\frac{\Delta ATC}{\Delta Q} = 0$, $Q = \sqrt{20} = 4.47$.

13. No. A firm frequently can make more money by serving a broader market.

14.

Output	TC	MC	AC
1	45	dna	45
2	54	9	27
3	67	13	22.33333
4	84	17	21

CASE TWO

A Managerial Application of Cost Functions by a Railroad
Edwin Mansfield and Harold H. Wein

There have been numerous studies where the relationship between cost and output has been estimated for manufacturing plants. These studies fall generally into two categories. In the first category, the chief purpose of the work has been to accumulate evidence concerning various cost curves that occupy an important place in economics. In the second category, the work has been done primarily with a view toward the direct usefulness of the relationship of cost and output to industrial managers. This paper falls into the second category.

We give an illustration here of how such a relationship may be used to formulate a simple control chart for costs, a topic which should be of interest to many applied statisticians and industrial managers. The problem of controlling performance and costs is important in almost every sector of industry and trade. Our data, and hence our specific results, pertain to the American railroad industry, but the statistical techniques that are used may be applicable to other industries as well.

FREIGHT YARDS AND COST CONTROL

Freight yards differ greatly in size, layout, and type, but they have certain physical characteristics and functions in common.

Physical Characteristics. All yards contain sets of tracks. In large yards they are generally of three types: receiving tracks where incoming freight cars are stored, classification tracks where cars are switched, and outbound tracks where cars that were situated on a classification track are stored until a locomotive hauls them away as a train.

Functions. Freight yards switch cars. That is, they sort incoming cars by putting them on the appropriate classification tracks, and in this way they break up incoming trains to form new trains. Most yards also deliver and pick up cars. Engines are assigned to deliver cars to industrial sidings and other yards and to pick them up there. Finally, many yards bill and inspect freight cars and perform such ancillary services as maintenance, repair, and storage.

Mansfield and Wein, "A Regression Control Chart for Cost," from *Applied Statistics* (Blackwell Publishers).

The importance of freight yards to a railroad is illustrated by the fact that about one-third of its total operating costs may arise in these yards. In view of this, it is clearly important that proper control be maintained over the performance of the yards. However, this problem of maintaining adequate control is made difficult by their number and their distribution over a large area. (For example, in the railroad we studied, about 200 freight yards are scattered along approximately 12,000 miles of track.) It is virtually impossible for any team of managers to have each day a reasonably complete knowledge of what happened at each yard. They must examine selected data concerning the performance of the yards during the day, and from these data they must somehow evaluate a yard's performance. In evaluating performance, one piece of information that is used is the costs incurred in the yard during the day.

At present, the data and techniques used by most railroads do not seem well suited for their purpose. Judging by the opinions of the railroad management with which we worked, their purpose is to detect those days when the costs at a yard are unusually high for the output produced and those series of days when the costs are repeatedly higher than would be expected. Detection of either of these would result in an inquiry concerning the causes of the apparent deterioration of yard performance. In addition, the management is interested in detecting days when costs are unusually low or when they are repeatedly lower than would be expected. In this case there would also be an inquiry, but the intention would be to encourage the responsible factors rather than to remedy them.

In this paper we discuss a control chart based on the relationship between cost and output that may be useful for these purposes. Before discussing the chart, it seems worthwhile to describe the measures of freight-yard output and costs that are used. The two most important services performed at a yard are switching and delivery; and it seems reasonable to use the number of "cuts" switched and the number of cars delivered during a particular period as a measure of output. A "cut" is a group of cars that rolls as a unit on to the same classification track; it is often used as a measure of switching output. The number of cars delivered includes both the cars delivered to sidings and other yards and those that are picked up. This output measure is not ideal, one difficulty being that it conceals considerable heterogeneity. For example, two groups of cars may be delivered but one may be hauled a greater distance than the other. Some of this heterogeneity could be eliminated by further refinements in the output measure, but the extra complexity with regard to data collection and computation might result in a loss of feasibility.

The costs used here include all money costs incurred in the yard except fixed charges, repair costs, maintenance and storage costs, and vacation costs. Only money costs are included; the costs that may be imputed to car delay are not taken into account. Fixed charges are excluded, but some of the included costs are essentially fixed in the very short run.

THE CONTROL CHART

The control chart contains the deviation of actual cost from the cost that would be expected on the basis of the average relationship between cost and output. These deviations are used to detect days when costs are suspiciously high or low. The model that underlies the chart is as follows: for a particular yard, the expected cost on the i'th day (C_i) is assumed to be a linear function of the number of cuts switched on the i'th day (S_i) and the number of cars delivered on the i'th day (D_i).

When the railroad management refers to unusually high or low costs, it seems clear that they mean costs that are unusual if the cost-output relationship and effects of numerous small disturbances remain at their previous, satisfactory levels. That is, they are interested in detecting those C_i that are unusually high or low if the average relationship between cost and output is unchanged. Similarly, when they refer to a sequence of days when costs are higher or lower than would be expected, it seems clear that they mean a run of the C_i that is unlikely if this relationship is unchanged.

If the model is adequate and if the average relationship between cost and output is known, it is a simple matter to set up a control chart that will aid the management. Each day, the deviation of actual cost from the cost that would be expected on the basis of this relationship can be plotted on a chart that has two sets of control limits. The outer control limits can be set so that, if this relationship remains the same, the probability that a point lies outside them is small. The inner control limits can be set so that, if this relationship remains the same, the probability that two consecutive points lie outside them (in one direction) is small. When a point lies outside the outer limits or a pair of points lies outside the inner limits, there is evidence that the relationship may have changed and that an inquiry should be made.

SETTING UP THE CHART

A control chart was set up at a freight yard located at Toledo, Ohio. This yard constitutes one of the largest and most important links in the railroad we studied. The chief types of freight that pass through the yard are livestock, perishables, coal, and automobiles. Table 1 shows the number of cars switched, the number of cuts switched, the number of cars delivered, the number of crews employed, the number of engine hours used, and the costs at the yard, for a sample one-week period.

The first step in setting up the chart was to gather historical data concerning cost and output. Data similar to those in Table 1 were collected for sixty-one days, and the average relationship between cost and output was estimated. The resulting relationship was

$$C_i = 4{,}914 + 0.42S_i + 2.44D_i \quad (1)$$

The second step was to test some of the assumptions underlying the chart. Some of these tests are quite similar to those used in quality control to determine if the process is "in control." Taken together, the results of these tests did not cast any great suspicion on the assumptions underlying the chart. Indeed, the results seemed to be quite compatible with these assumptions.

The third step was to draw the inner and outer control limits on the chart. The outer control limits were set at $\pm\$804$, and the inner control limits were set at $\pm\$410$. These limits (designated by ICL and OCL) are included in Figure 1. If there were no errors in the assumptions, the probability

TABLE 1   **Output, Cost, and Employment, Freight Yard, Toledo, 7 Days***

ITEM	FRI.	SAT.	SUN.	MON.	TUES.	WED.	THURS.
Number of cuts switched	869	792	762	586	669	732	659
Number of cars switched	2534	2303	2521	1849	2090	2114	1979
Number of cars delivered[†]	1015	1003	820	548	877	706	1038
Number of crews used	45	45	40	38	46	46	46
Number of engine hours	372	369	329	309	385	381	386
Money costs ($)	7523	7464	6932	6550	7606	7757	7701

* Taken from records of cooperating railroad.
[†] Includes number of cars picked up.

FIGURE 1
Deviation of Actual Cost from Expected Cost Based on Average Relationship between Cost and Output: Freight Yard, 61 Days

Source: Records of cooperating railroad.

would be 0.05 that a point would lie outside the outer limits if the relationship remained fixed. Similarly, the probability would be about 0.03 that two consecutive points would lie outside the same inner control limit.

After setting the control limits, an attempt was made to determine if any assignable cause could be found for the days that were "out of control." None could be found, and it was assumed that they were due to "chance." The number of such days was almost precisely what one would expect on a chance basis.

PERFORMANCE OF THE CHART

This section describes the performance of the chart during a six-week period that was several months subsequent to the time when the chart was set up. The results

apply to the freight yard described above. On each day during the period data were collected concerning the money costs (C), the number of cuts switched (S), and the number of cars delivered (D) on the previous day. Then the deviation of actual cost from expected cost based on the average relationship in equation (1) was computed and plotted on the chart.[1] The deviations that were plotted are shown in Figure 2.

During the six-week period, four days seemed to be out of control, and in every case there seemed to be an assignable cause. One of these days was Labor Day. The exceptionally high costs on Labor Day can be attributed to the punitive wage-rates that were paid because it was a holiday. On the other days that were out of control (all of them Sundays) the exceptionally low costs can be attributed in part to the following circumstances: (1) Cars delivered to other yards constituted a large proportion

---

[1]Actually, the relationship was recomputed as more and more data became available.

FIGURE 2
Control Chart for Costs: Freight Yard, 42 Days

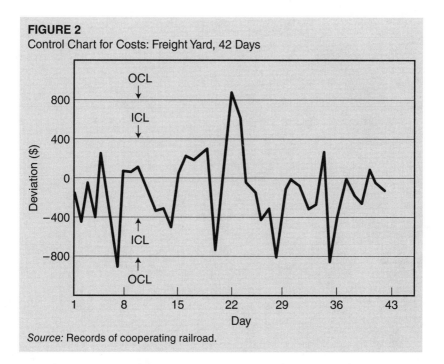

Source: Records of cooperating railroad.

of all cars delivered, and since such cars are relatively easy to deliver, costs were depressed. (2) More efficient methods were used to handle incoming cars. (3) Some work ordinarily performed by the yard was done by another yard; hence costs were reduced somewhat.

The basic data were collected by railroad employees and the points on the chart were computed by officials of the railroad. From their evaluation of the performance of the yard it appeared that the chart provided a reasonably faithful picture of the level of performance. Moreover, the chart stimulated some inquiries that indicated where improvements in yard performance might be made.

Questions

1. Do managers often find it difficult to minimize costs? If so, why?

2. Can control charts of the sort described in this case help managers to minimize costs? If so, how?

3. Is equation (1) a short-run or long-run cost function? Why?

4. What is the marginal cost of switching a cut?

5. What is the marginal cost of delivering a car?

6. Does the average cost per cut switched exceed the marginal cost of switching a cut?

7. In what ways can these estimates of marginal and average cost be useful to railroad managers? Explain.

Part Four
MARKET STRUCTURE AND
SIMPLE PRICING STRATEGIES

CHAPTER 6

Perfect Competition

Chapter Profile

A **perfectly competitive** firm will set its output so that price equals marginal cost. If there exists an output rate where price exceeds average variable costs, it will pay the firm to produce, even though price does not cover average total costs. But if there does not exist an output rate where price exceeds average variable costs, the firm is better off to produce nothing at all. In the long run, the firm will produce at the minimum point on its long-run average total cost curve. Price tends to be at the level where the market demand curve intersects the market supply curve. The perfectly competitive firm, therefore, is a price taker, the price being set by the marketplace.

The producer surplus is the difference between the market price and the price the producer is willing to receive for the good or service (the producer's reservation price). This reservation price for a firm in a perfectly competitive market is the marginal cost but only when the marginal cost is above the break-even point for that firm. When combined with the consumer surplus, a measure of social welfare can be constructed and the distribution of this surplus among consumers and producers depends on the shape of the demand and supply curves.

A constant-cost industry has a horizontal long-run supply curve while an increasing-cost industry has a positively sloped long-run supply curve, which means that, as an increasing-cost industry expands over time, there will be an increase in the prices of input such as labor, capital, and new materials.

Key Formulas to Remember

1. Profits = total revenue less total cost:

$$\pi = TR - TC$$

2. Marginal revenue = marginal cost at the point where profits are maximized:

$$MR = MC, \text{ remembering that } MR = \frac{\Delta TR}{\Delta Q} \text{ and } MC = \frac{\Delta TC}{\Delta Q}$$

Questions

Completion

1. In the long run, a perfectly competitive firm's equilibrium position is at the place where its long-run average cost equals _____.

2. For a perfectly competitive firm in the long run, total cost of production equals $500,000. Given that the firm is producing and selling 100,000 units, equilibrium price equals _____.

3. In the short run, a firm will continue to produce, even at a loss, as long as the price exceeds _____.

4. The producer surplus for a perfectly competitive firm is the _____ of producing the good or service.

5. For a perfectly competitive firm, marginal revenue _____ price.

6. A horizontal long-run supply curve is characteristic of a _____ industry.

7. If a firm produces nothing, it must still pay its _____.

8. The demand curve for a perfectly competitive firm has a _____ shape.

9. A measure of brand loyalty is the percentage of customers buying a particular brand today that will buy this brand _____.

10. If the firm is operating in a perfectly competitive market at equilibrium, marginal cost _____ average cost of production.

True or False

____ 1. In the long run, equilibrium price under perfect competition may be above or below average total cost.

____ 2. Under perfect competition, one producer can produce a somewhat different good from other producers in the industry.

____ 3. Under perfect competition, each firm must be careful not to produce too much and spoil the market.

____ 4. At the equilibrium price, price will equal marginal cost (for all firms that choose to produce) under perfect competition.

____ 5. A perfectly competitive firm cannot change its prices or output, even in the long run.

Multiple Choice

1. The market demand curve for a particular kind of table is as follows:

Price (dollars)	Quantity demanded
30	200
20	300
10	400
5	600
3	800

The industry producing this kind of table has a horizontal long-run supply curve, and each firm has the following long-run total cost curve:

Output	Total cost (dollars)
1	10
2	12
3	15
4	30

(Each firm can produce only integer numbers of units of output.)
In the long run, the total number of firms in this industry will be about:

a. 100
b. 200
c. 300
d. 400
e. 500

2. The long-run average cost curve of the Longacre Company, a perfectly competitive firm, follows. Given that this curve does not shift, the long-run equilibrium output of this firm will be:

a. 4 units
b. 5 units
c. 6 units
d. 7 units
e. 8 units

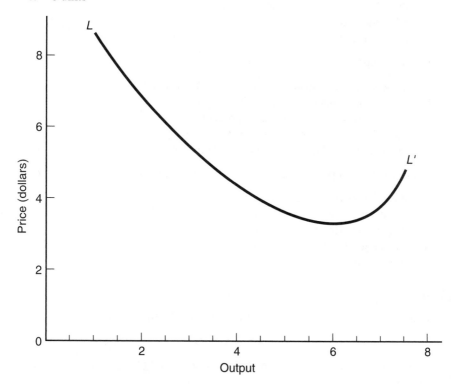

3. The total cost and total revenue of the Connors Company, a perfectly competitive firm, follow:

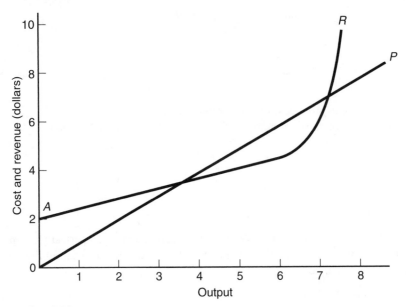

The line $0P$ is:

a. the total cost curve
b. the total revenue curve
c. the relationship between price and output
d. all of the above
e. none of the above

4. Perfect competition is where there are:

a. a few specialized firms producing the same product
b. a few firms producing many different products
c. many firms producing different products
d. many firms producing two products
e. many firms producing a standardized product

5. In the short run, a perfectly competitive firm will shut down when:

a. it is not covering its fixed costs
b. it is not covering its average variable costs
c. it is not covering its total costs
d. when both a and b occur
e. when both b and c occur

Problems

1. In the cotton textile industry, each firm's marginal cost curve is

$$MC = 5 + 3Q$$

where MC is its marginal cost (in dollars per ton), and Q is its output per day (in tons).

a. If there are 1,000 firms in the cotton textile industry, derive the industry's short-run supply curve.

b. If the price is $8, how much will the cotton textile industry produce per day?

c. Can you derive each firm's total cost function? Why or why not?

2. Each firm in a perfectly competitive industry has the short-run total cost function that follows.

Output	Total cost (dollars)
0	10
1	12
2	16
3	22
4	30
5	40

There are 1,000 firms in this industry, and the market demand curve is as follows:

Price (dollars)	Quantity demanded
3	3,000
5	2,000
7	1,500
9	1,000

a. What is the equilibrium price of the product? (Assume that the price must be $3, $5, $7, or $9.)

b. What will be the output of each firm?

c. If you were considering investing in this industry, would you forecast that, in the long run, firms would tend to enter or leave this industry?

3. The Jackson Company, a perfectly competitive firm, has the following total cost function:

Total output	Total cost (dollars)
0	20
1	30
2	42
3	55
4	69
5	84
6	100
7	117

How much will the Jackson Company produce, if the price is:

a. $13
b. $14
c. $15
d. $16
e. $17

4. The Murphy Corporation's marginal cost curve is

$$MC = 4 + 3Q$$

where MC is the cost (in dollars) of producing the Qth unit of its product, and Q is the number of units of its product produced per day. The price of a unit of its product is $3. A consultant hired by the Murphy Corporation argues that, based on this evidence, the firm would make more money by shutting down than by continuing to operate. Do you agree? Explain.

5. The Landau Company's average cost curve is

$$AC = \frac{400}{Q} + 3Q$$

where AC is its average cost (in dollars), and Q is the number of units of its product that is produced per day. The price of a unit of its product is $3, regardless of how many units it sells.

 a. If the firm produces more than 1 unit per day, is it making profits or losses? Explain.
 b. Is the firm better off to shut down or operate? Explain.

6. In the early 1950s, it was proposed that New York subway fares should be increased. William Vickrey of Columbia University was asked by the Mayor's Committee on Management Survey of the City of New York to make a study to help evaluate the proposal. Vickrey estimated the demand curve; part of his results follow. How would these data be useful in deciding whether or not to raise the subway fare from the then-prevailing level of 10 cents? What additional data would you need in order to come to a conclusion on this score? Do you think that data of this sort would be as useful now as in the early 1950s?

Fare (cents)	Passengers	Total revenue (dollars)
5	1,945	$ 97.2
10	1,683	168.3
15	1,421	213.2
20	1,159	231.8
25	897	224.2
30	635	190.5

Source: W. S. Vickrey. Passengers and revenues are in millions per year.

7. The Rosemont Company is a member of a perfectly competitive industry. Like all members of the industry, its total cost function is

$$TC = 160{,}000 + 100Q + 4Q^2$$

where TC is the firm's monthly total cost (in dollars), and Q is the firm's monthly output.

 a. If the industry is in long-run equilibrium, what is the price of the Rosemont Company's product?
 b. What is the firm's monthly output?

8. The London Corporation's total cost function (where TC is total cost in dollars, and Q is quantity) is

$$TC = 400 + 6Q + 3Q^2$$

   a. If the firm is perfectly competitive and if the price of its product is $36, what is its optimal output rate?
   b. At this output rate, what are its profits?

9. The supply and demand curves for a product are as follows:

$$Q_S = 10,000P$$
$$Q_D = 25,000 - 15,000P$$

   where Q_S is the quantity (tons) supplied, Q_D is the quantity (tons) demanded, and P is the price per ton (in hundreds of dollars per ton).

   a. What is the equilibrium price?
   b. What is the equilibrium quantity?

Answers

Completion
1. price   2. $5   3. average variable cost   4. marginal cost   5. equals
6. constant cost   7. fixed cost   8. horizontal   9. again when next they buy the product   10. equals

True or False
1. False   2. False   3. False   4. True   5. False

Multiple Choice
1. b   2. c   3. b   4. e   5. e

Problems
1. a. If Q is the quantity supplied by the industry (in tons per day) and P is the price (in dollars per ton),

$$Q = \frac{-5,000}{3} + \frac{1,000P}{3}$$

   b. 1,000 tons
   c. No.

2. a. $5
   b. 2 units
   c. They will tend to leave this industry.

3. The Jackson Company's marginal cost curve is

Output	Marginal cost (dollars)
0 to 1	10
1 to 2	12
2 to 3	13
3 to 4	14
4 to 5	15
5 to 6	16
6 to 7	17

   a. If the price is $13, the Jackson Company will produce 2 or 3 units.
   b. 3 or 4 units
   c. 4 or 5 units
   d. 5 or 6 units
   e. 6 or 7 units

4. According to this evidence, the marginal cost of the first unit of output is $4 + (3)(1) = \$7$. Clearly, if the price of a unit of the product is $3, the firm loses money on each unit it sells. Indeed, it does not even cover its variable costs. Thus, the consultant is right; the firm should produce nothing.

5. a. The firm's total cost function is

$$C = AC \cdot Q = \left[\frac{400}{Q} + 3Q\right]Q = 400 + 3Q^2$$

The firm's total revenue equals $R = 3Q$. Thus, its profit equals

$$\pi = R - C = 3Q - 400 - 3Q^2 = -400 - 3(Q^2 - Q) = -400 - 3Q(Q - 1)$$

If $Q > 1$, the firm incurs losses because $\pi = -400 - 3Q(Q - 1)$ is negative.
   b. Since $\pi = -400 - 3Q(Q - 1)$, the maximum value of π is not achieved at $Q = 0$. For example, if $Q = 1/2$, $\pi = -400 - 3(1/2)(-1/2) = -399\frac{1}{4}$. This is a higher value of π than -400, which is the value of π when $Q = 0$. Thus, assuming that the firm can produce fractional units of output per day, it is better off to operate than to shut down.

6. The demand for subway travel is shown by the table to be price inelastic at the then-prevailing fare of 10 cents. This means that increases in the fare would increase total revenues. Also, they would reduce the subway deficit because fewer passengers would mean lower costs (or at least no higher costs). But this is not the only consideration. You would probably want to investigate how such a fare increase would affect various parts of the population—the poor, the rich, rush-hour traffic, non-rush-hour traffic, and so on. Data of this sort would be just as relevant now as in the early 1950s.

7. a. Average cost equals

$$AC = \frac{160,000}{Q} + 100 + 4Q$$

Thus, the minimum value of average cost occurs when

$$\frac{\Delta AC}{\Delta Q} = \frac{-160{,}000}{Q^2} + 4 = 0$$

Substituting 200 for Q in the equation for average cost, the minimum value of average cost equals

$$\frac{160{,}000}{200} + 100 + 4(200) = 1{,}700$$

Thus, in the long run, price equals $1,700.
  b. 200

8. a. Since marginal cost equals

$$MC = \frac{\Delta TC}{\Delta Q} = 6 + 6Q$$

marginal cost equals price when

$$6 + 6Q = 36$$
$$Q = 5$$

Thus, the optimal output rate is 5 units.
  b. $5(36) - [400 + 6(5) + 3(25)] = 180 - 505 = -325$

9. a. Since QD must equal QS,

$$10{,}000P = 25{,}000 - 15{,}000P$$
$$P = 1$$

  b. 10,000 tons

CHAPTER 7

Monopoly and Monopolistic Competition

Chapter Profile

Under **monopoly**, a firm will maximize profit if it sets its output rate at the point where marginal revenue equals marginal cost. However, there is no guarantee that a firm that holds a monopoly over the production of a particular product must make a profit. If the monopolist cannot cover its variable costs, it, like a perfectly competitive firm, will shut down, even in the short run.

Empirical studies indicate that firms frequently use cost-plus pricing. In this approach, the firm estimates the cost per unit of output of the product (based on some assumed output level) and adds a markup to include costs that cannot be allocated to any specific product and to provide a return on the firm's investment. On the surface, it is questionable whether this approach can maximize profit, but if marginal cost (not average cost) is really what is being marked up, and if the markup is determined (in the appropriate way) by the price elasticity of demand of the product, **cost-plus pricing** can result in profit maximization.

Firms generally produce and sell more than one product. It is important for them to recognize the demand interrelationships among the products they sell. Also, a firm's products are often interrelated in production. If two products are produced jointly in fixed proportions, the profit-maximizing output is where the total marginal revenue curve—the vertical summation of the marginal revenue curves for the individual products—intersects the marginal cost curve for the bundle of products (assuming that the marginal revenue of each product is nonnegative).

If two products are produced jointly in variable proportions, one can construct isocost curves, each of which shows the combinations of outputs that can be produced at the same total cost. Also, isorevenue lines can be constructed, each of which shows the combinations of outputs that yield the same total revenue. For an output combination to be optimal, it must be at a point where an **isorevenue line** is tangent to an **isocost curve**. To determine which output combination is optimal, one compares the profit levels at the tangency points. The tangency point where profit is highest is the optimal output combination.

Monopsony occurs when there is only one buyer and the **monopsonist** controls the price. A firm can be both a monopolist as well as a monopsonist, although this is not a typical occurrence.

In contrast to perfect competition, where all firms sell an identical product, firms under **monopolistic competition** sell somewhat different products. Producers differentiate their product from that of other producers. Thus, the demand curve facing each firm slopes downward to the right—and is not horizontal, as it would be under perfect competition. Each firm will set marginal revenue equal to marginal cost. In the long run, each firm will produce to the left of the minimum point on its long-run average total cost curve.

Monopolistically competitive firms spend very large amounts on advertising. To maximize its profits, a firm should set its advertising so that the marginal revenue from an extra dollar of advertising equals the price elasticity of demand. A graph showing how both the price elasticity and the marginal revenue from an extra dollar of advertising vary with the amount spent by the firm on advertising can shed useful light on this topic.

Advertising of price changes may increase the price elasticity of demand for the product whose price is changed. This is because advertising makes more consumers aware of the price changes. Measures of brand loyalty are useful in guiding decisions concerning promotional activities to increase sales of particular brands.

Key Formulas to Remember

1. When marginal revenue equals marginal cost ($MR = MC$), marginal revenue can also be represented as MR $also = P = \dfrac{MC}{\left[1 + \left(\dfrac{1}{\eta}\right)\right]}$, remembering that η is elasticity of demand and that it has a negative value.

2. Markup equals:

$$\frac{(\text{price} - \text{cost})}{\text{cost}}$$

    where (price − cost) is the profit margin, and therefore,

$$\text{Price} = \text{cost}(1 + \text{markup})$$

3. Pricing with a target return:

$$P = L + M + K + \left[\frac{F}{Q}\right] + \left[\frac{\pi A}{Q}\right]$$

    where P is price, L is unit of labor cost, M is unit material cost, K is unit marketing cost, F is total fixed or indirect costs, Q is the number of units the firm plans to produce, A is total gross operating assets, and π is desired profits on these assets.

Questions

Completion

1. A monopolist can sell 12 units of output when it charges $8 a unit, 11 units of output when it charges $9 a unit, and 10 units of output when it charges $10 a unit. The marginal revenue from the eleventh unit of output equals _____. The marginal revenue from the twelfth unit of output equals _____.

2. A monopolist's demand curve is the same as the industry _____.

3. For a monopolist, marginal revenue is _____ than price.

4. Price will be _____ under monopoly than under perfect competition.

5. Output will be _____ under monopoly than under perfect competition.

6. A monopolistically competitive firm is in long-run equilibrium. Its marginal revenue equals $10. If its marginal revenue plus its economic profit equals one-half of its price, its price equals _____, and its marginal cost equals _____.

7. If two products are produced jointly in fixed proportions, the profit-maximizing output is where the _____ of the marginal revenue curves of the individual products intersects the _____ for the bundle of products.

8. The statement in the previous question assumes that the marginal revenue of each product is _____.

9. If the Johnstown Company produces 1 unit of good X, it automatically produces 2 units of good Y. Goods X and Y are _____ products produced in _____ proportions.

10. From a production point of view, goods X and Y (in the previous question) are not separate products but should be viewed as a(n) _____.

True or False

_____ 1. A profit-maximizing monopolist will always choose an output in the short run where average total cost is less than average revenue.

_____ 2. A monopolist always produces an output such that the price elasticity of demand is −1.

_____ 3. A monopolistically competitive firm's short-run demand and cost curves are as follows:

Price (dollars)	Quantity demanded	Output	Total cost (dollars)
8	1	1	5
7	2	2	7
6	3	3	9
4	4	4	11
3	5	5	20

This firm, if it maximizes profit, will choose an output rate of 5.

_____ 4. If a firm is maximizing profit, the percentage markup on a product is directly related to the product's price elasticity of demand.

_____ 5. A profit-maximizing multiple-plant monopolist will allocate production equally across locations.

_____ 6. To maximize profit, a firm with two plants (A and B) will allocate output between them so that the average cost at plant A equals the average cost at plant B.

_____ 7. Surveys of business-pricing practices show that few firms use cost-plus pricing.

_____ 8. If marginal cost is what is being marked up and if the markup (in absolute terms) equals $MC(1 + 1/n)$, the firm can maximize profit.

_____ 9. If two goods are joint products, they must be produced in variable proportions.

_____ 10. In monopolistic competition, only a very small number of firms produce a standardized product.

Multiple Choice

1. A monopolist's total cost equals $100 + 3Q$, where Q is the number of units of output it produces per month. Its demand curve is $P = 200 – Q$, where P is the price of the product. The marginal revenue from the twentieth unit of output per month equals:

   a. $3,600
   b. $3,439
   c. $180
   d. $140
   e. none of the above

2. A monopolistic firm will expand its output when:

   a. marginal revenue exceeds marginal cost
   b. marginal cost exceeds marginal revenue
   c. marginal cost equals marginal revenue
   d. marginal revenue is negative
   e. none of the above

3. A profit-maximizing firm, if it owns a number of plants, will always:

   a. produce some of its output at each plant
   b. transfer output from plants with high marginal cost to those with low marginal cost
   c. transfer output from plants with low marginal cost to those with high marginal cost
   d. produce all of its output at a single plant and shut down the rest
   e. none of the above

4. A monopolistically competitive firm is operating at a point where its marginal cost of production equals its average cost of production. The firm:

   a. is in long-run equilibrium
   b. should increase its level of production
   c. should lower its price
   d. is experiencing negative economic profits
   e. none of the above

5. If the price elasticity of demand for a product equals –2 and if its producer wants to maximize profit, its marginal cost should be marked up by:

    a. 50 percent
    b. 100 percent
    c. 150 percent
    d. 200 percent
    e. none of the above

6. If the price elasticity of demand for a product equals –3 and if its producer wants to maximize profit, its price should be:

    a. double its average cost
    b. 150 percent of its average cost
    c. double its marginal cost
    d. 150 percent of its marginal cost
    e. none of the above

Problems

1. The Ardmore Company's marginal cost of production is zero if its output is less than (or equal to) 40 units per day.

    a. If its output rate is 20 units per day, does its average total cost exceed its average fixed cost?
    b. If the Ardmore Company is a perfectly competitive firm, will it produce less than 40 units per day? Why or why not?
    c. If the Ardmore Company is a monopolist, under what conditions (if ever), will it produce less than 40 units per day? Explain.

2. The Towne Food Corporation has bought exclusive rights to sell chocolate bars in a local sports arena. The fee it paid for this concession was $1,000 per game. The cost (excluding this fee) of obtaining and marketing each candy bar is 10 cents. The demand schedule for candy bars in this arena is as follows:

Price per candy bar (cents)	Thousands of candy bars sold per game
20	10
25	9
30	8
35	7
40	6
45	5
50	4

    It is assumed that prices must be multiples of a nickel.

    a. What price should the Towne Food Corporation charge for a candy bar?
    b. What is the maximum amount that the Towne Food Corporation should pay for this concession for a single game?

3. Beer manufacturers try to differentiate their products by advertising and other means. In recent decades, there has been a reduction in the number of beer

producers: in 1947, there were 404; in 1963, 150; and in 1974, 58. The rate of return, after taxes, on owner's equity in this industry was usually below 8 percent in the post–World War II period, but it increased to 9.1 percent in 1967, 10.1 percent in 1969, and 8.8 percent in 1971. For all manufacturing, the comparable rate of return in 1967, 1969, and 1971 was 11.7, 11.5, and 9.7 percent, respectively.

    a.   Would you characterize the beer industry in the United States as monopolistically competitive? Why or why not?

    b.   With regard to production differentiation, does it have the characteristics of a monopolistically competitive industry?

    c.   Is its profit performance similar to what would be expected in a monopolistically competitive industry?

    d.   Do you think that it is becoming closer to monopolistic competition than it used to be? Why or why not?

4.   The Haas Company believes that the price elasticity of demand for its product equals –2. It also believes that an extra $1 million in advertising would increase its sales by $1.5 million.

    a.   Is the Haas Company spending the optimal amount on advertising? Why or why not?

    b.   If not, should it spend more or less on advertising? Explain.

5.   For the Schmidt Company, the marginal revenue from an extra dollar of advertising is as follows.

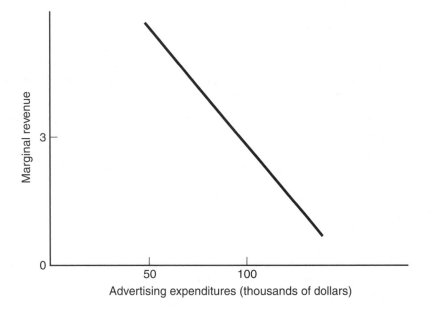

If the price elasticity of demand for the Schmidt Company's product is –3, regardless of how much is spent on advertising, how much should the firm spend on advertising?

6.   The Nibelungen Company, an unregulated monopoly, finds that its marginal cost curve is $MC = 80 + 4Q$, where MC is marginal cost (in dollars), and Q is output.

The demand curve for its product is $P = 200 - 2Q$, where P is the product price (in dollars), and Q is output.

   a. If this firm wants to maximize profit, what output should it choose?
   b. What price should it charge?

7. The Garfield Company's marketing manager believes that the price elasticity of demand for its product equals -1.8, and that the relationship between the amount spent by the firm on advertising and its sales is as follows:

Advertising expenditure	Sales
$200,000	$0.6 million
300,000	0.9 million
400,000	1.1 million
500,000	1.2 million

   a. If the Garfield Company is spending $300,000 on advertising, what is the marginal revenue from an extra dollar of advertising?
   b. Is $300,000 the optimal amount for the firm to spend on advertising?
   c. If $300,000 is not the optimal amount, would you recommend that the firm spend more or less on advertising?

8. The Montana Company estimates its average total cost to be $22 per unit of output when it produces 15,000 units, which it regards as 75 percent of capacity. It wants to earn 20 percent on its total investment, which is $175,000.

   a. If it uses cost-plus pricing, what price should it set?
   b. What percentage markup will it use?

9. The Dakota Company's total annual indirect costs (for all products) are estimated to be $3 million, and its total annual variable costs (for all products) are estimated to be $1.5 million. Indirect costs are allocated among the firm's products on the basis of their average variable costs.

   a. If the average variable cost of product X is $14, how much would the firm add on for indirect cost?
   b. What would the estimated fully allocated cost per unit be for product X?
   c. If the markup for product X is 50 percent, what will its price be?

Answers

Completion
1. –$1, –$3 2. demand curve 3. less 4. higher 5. lower 6. $20, $10
7. vertical summation, marginal cost curve 8. nonnegative 9. joint, fixed
10. bundle

True or False
1. False 2. False 3. False 4. False 5. False 6. False 7. False
8. False 9. False 10. False

Multiple Choice

1. e   2. a   3. b   4. d   5. b   6. d

Problems

1. a. No. They are equal.
    b. No, since marginal cost (which is zero) must be less than price (unless it too is zero).
    c. It will produce less than 40 units per day if marginal revenue equals zero (and thus is equal to marginal cost) at an output less than 40 units per day.

2. a. Since total cost (excluding the fee) is 10 cents times the number of candy bars sold, the Towne Food Corporation's total profit per game (before paying the fee) is shown below, under various assumptions concerning the price.

Thousands of candy bars	Price (cents)	Total revenue (dollars)	Total cost (dollars) (excluding fee)	Total profit (dollars)
10	20	2,000	1,000	1,000
9	25	2,250	900	1,350
8	30	2,400	800	1,600
7	35	2,450	700	1,750
6	40	2,400	600	1,800
5	45	2,250	500	1,750
4	50	2,000	400	1,600

   Thus, the Towne Food Corporation will maximize profit if it sets a price of 40 cents.
    b. $1,800, since this is the maximum amount it could make per game.

3. a. The beer industry has some characteristics of monopolistic competition, but it departs from it in other respects. In a particular geographical market, there may be a limited number of beers that are distributed. In contrast, monopolistic competition occurs where there are a great many sellers. Also, the barriers to entry in the beer industry are not inconsiderable, whereas monopolistic competition assumes free entry.
    b. Yes, the beer industry is characterized by product differentiation.
    c. Its profits have not been above average. In this respect, at least, its profit performance is similar to a monopolistically competitive industry.
    d. No, because the number of breweries has declined, and it seems to be increasingly oligopolistic.

4. a. No. It should set the marginal revenue from an extra dollar of its advertising equal to its price elasticity of demand.
    b. Less.

5. $100,000

    a. Setting marginal cost equal to marginal revenue,
    $$80 + 4Q = 200 - 4Q$$
    $$Q = 15$$

    b. $P = 200 - 2(15) = 170$

7. a. 2
   b. No.
   c. More.

8. a. To earn 20 percent on its investment of $175,000, its profit must be $35,000. Thus, the per-unit markup must be $35,000 ÷ 15,000 = $2.33, and the price must equal $22 + $2.33 = $24.33.
   b. $2.33 ÷ $22 = 10.6 percent.

9. a. $28
   b. $42
   c. $63

Part Five

SOPHISTICATED MARKET PRICING

CHAPTER 8

Managerial Use of Price Discrimination

Chapter Profile

Price discrimination occurs when the same commodity is sold at more than one price. A firm can increase profits and capture more of the consumer surplus through price discrimination. A firm will be able and willing to practice price discrimination if various classes of buyers with different price elasticities of demand can be identified and segregated and if the commodity cannot be transferred easily from one class to another.

Economists divide price discrimination into three types. **First-degree price discrimination** occurs when a firm can charge each customer his or her reservation price (which, therefore, will capture all of the consumer surplus and convert it to producer surplus). Managers sell to consumers as long as the reservation price exceeds the marginal cost of production. **Second-degree price discrimination** prices increments of output at different rates, charging a high price for the first increments of output and then lower prices as consumers' consumption increases. This is commonly used in public utility pricing, where, for example, electricity will be priced higher for customers who purchase small quantities and lower for customers purchasing more. Finally, **third-degree price discrimination** can occur when the total market is divided into heterogeneous classes where each segment can be identified, has different elasticities of demand, and can be separated (excluded) from the other segments. The firm will then be able to maximize its profits by choosing prices and outputs so that the marginal revenue in each class is equal to marginal cost.

One technique for implementing first-degree price discrimination is a **two-part tariff**, which consists of an entry fee and a use fee. The entry fee is designed to capture the consumer surplus, and the use fee reflects the marginal cost.

Questions

Completion

1. If a firm is maximizing profit, the percentage markup on a product is (directly, inversely) _____ related to the product's price elasticity of demand.

2. The price at which one division of a firm sells to another division is the _____ price.

3. If there is a perfectly competitive market for the transferred product, the transfer price should equal the _____.

4. If two products are produced jointly in fixed proportions, the profit-maximizing output is where the _____ of the marginal revenue curves of the individual products intersects the _____ for the bundle of products.

5. The statement in the previous question assumes that the marginal revenue of each product is _____.

6. If the Johnstown Company produces 1 unit of good X, it automatically produces 2 units of good Y. Goods X and Y are _____ products produced in _____ proportions.

7. From a production point of view, goods X and Y (in the previous question) are not separate products but should be viewed as a(n) _____.

8. A price-discriminating firm will charge _____ to a customer with a greater price elasticity than to another customer.

9. The price-setting behavior of automobile salespeople is an example of _____-degree price discrimination.

True or False

_____ 1. Price discrimination is unlikely to occur unless consumers can be segregated into classes and the commodity cannot be transferred from one class to another.

_____ 2. Price discrimination always occurs when differences in price exist among roughly similar products, even when their costs are not the same.

_____ 3. Price discrimination is profitable even when the price elasticity of demand is the same among each class of consumer in the total market.

_____ 4. If a monopoly practices price discrimination, it does not set marginal revenue equal to marginal cost.

_____ 5. First-degree price discrimination occurs frequently, particularly in the auto industry.

_____ 6. Mass coupons and rebates allow a firm to practice first-degree price discrimination.

_____ 7. Charging two different prices for the same good at different locations is an example of price discrimination.

_____ 8. To maximize profits, the optimal two-part tariff charges the marginal cost as the use fee and the resulting consumer surplus as the entry fee.

Multiple Choice

1. For first-degree price discrimination to occur, a firm must have:

   a. an infinite number of buyers
   b. knowledge of the maximum prices buyers are willing to accept
   c. a small number of buyers

    d.   both a and b

    e.   both b and c

2.   Second-degree price discrimination is:

    a.   more common than first-degree price discrimination

    b.   often practiced by electric and gas companies

    c.   a way for sellers to increase their profits

    d.   all of the above

    e.   none of the above

3.   To determine how a discriminating monopolist will allocate output between two classes of consumers, one must:

    a.   compare the marginal revenues in the classes

    b.   compare the prices in the classes

    c.   compare the slopes of the demand curves in the classes

    d.   compare the heights of the demand curves in the classes

    e.   none of the above

4.   When a football team, desiring to maximize revenues, requires season ticket holders to first purchase a "right" to a seat before they can purchase actual season tickets, the team is:

    a.   price discriminating

    b.   using a two-part tariff pricing mechanism

    c.   tying

    d.   attempting to capture all of the consumer surplus

    e.   all of the above

5.   An electric utility typically charges home owners different rates than industrial users. The utility is:

    a.   price discriminating

    b.   reflecting the different costs of delivering electricity to different users

    c.   accurately estimating the different demand curves of its customers

    d.   all of the above

    e.   none of the above

Problems

1.   The Logan Company sells in two distinct markets, which are sealed off from each other. The demand curve for the firm's output in the one market is

$$P_1 = 200 - 10Q_1$$

where P_1 is the price of the product, and Q_1 is the amount sold in the first market. In the second market, the demand curve for the firm's product is

$$P_2 = 100 - 5Q_2$$

where P_2 is the price of the product, and Q_2 is the amount sold in the second market. The firm's marginal cost curve is

$$MC = 10Q$$

where Q is the firm's entire output.

    a. How many units should the firm sell in the first market?
    b. What price should it charge in the first market?
    c. How many units should the firm sell in the second market?
    d. What price should it charge in the second market?

2. The makers of methyl methacrylate used to sell it at 85 cents per pound for commercial purposes; for denture purposes, it was sold to the dental profession for
$45 per pound. Assuming that there was no difference in quality, why would the
producers of methyl methacrylate—DuPont and Rohm and Haas—find it profitable to charge different prices? In which of these markets (the commercial
market or the dental market) do you think the price elasticity of demand
was lower?

3. The Ohio Company sells a product with marginal cost equal to $9. If the Ohio
Company maximizes profit, what must be the price elasticity of demand for this
product if

    a. the product's price is $18?
    b. the product's price is $27?
    c. the product's price is $13.50?

4. The California Corporation is composed of a marketing division and a production
division. The marginal cost of producing a unit of the firm's product is $8 per unit,
and the marginal cost of marketing it is $6 per unit. The demand curve for the
firm's product is

$$P = 200 - 0.015Q$$

where P is the price per unit (in dollars), and Q is output (in units). There is no
external market for the good made by the production division.

    a. What is the California Corporation's optimal output?
    b. What price should it charge?
    c. How much should the production division charge the marketing division for
       each unit of the product?

5. The Beiswanger Company sells plastic toys in the United States and Europe.
According to the firm's marketing department, marginal revenue is $8 per unit
in both these markets. The firm's president says that it should sell more in
Europe and less in the United States. The vice president of marketing
disagrees.

    a. Who is right? (Assume that marginal cost is the same in the United States as
       in Europe.)
    b. Can you determine whether the price elasticity of demand is the same in both
       markets? Why or why not?
    c. Can you determine whether the price of the toy is the same in both markets?
       Why or why not?

6. Assume that a company can identify the price elasticity of demand for two different market segments for its product. The wealthier segment has a price elasticity of demand equal to –1.5, whereas the less affluent area has a price elasticity of demand equal to –3. Assuming a constant marginal cost of production of $4:

   a. What price should the firm set for its product?
   b. What should the amount of the coupon be?

Answers

Completion

1. inversely   2. transfer   3. price in the perfectly competitive market
4. vertical summation, marginal cost curve   5. nonnegative   6. joint, fixed   7. bundle   8. less   9. first

True or False

1. True   2. False   3. False   4. False   5. False   6. False   7. False   8. True

Multiple Choice

1. e   2. d   3. a   4. e   5. d

Problems

1. a. Since marginal revenue in the first market equals $200 - 20Q_1$, and marginal revenue in the second market equals $100 - 10Q_2$, it follows that

$$200 - 20Q_1 = 100 - 10Q_2 = 10(Q_1 + Q_2)$$

   Thus, $Q_1 = 10 - 2Q_2$, and $200 - 20(10 - 2Q_2) = 100 - 10Q_2$, which means that $Q_2 = 2$. Consequently, $Q_1 = 10 - 2(2)$, or 6.
   b. $200 - 10(6) = 140$
   c. 2
   d. $100 - 5(2) = 90$

2. Because the price elasticity of demand was different in the two markets. The dental market.

3. a. –2
   b. –1.5
   c. –3

4. a. Since the firm's marginal cost equals $8 + $6 = $14, and the firm's marginal revenue equals $200 - 0.03Q$, the profit-maximizing level of output is the one where

$$200 - 0.03Q = 14$$
$$Q = 6,200$$

   b. Price should equal $200 - 0.015(6,200) = 107.
   c. $8

5. a. The vice president of marketing.
   b. No, because marginal revenue depends both on the price elasticity of demand and price.
   c. No. See the answer to part b.

6. a. The firm should set price equal to $12 = 4 \cdot (-1.5/-0.5)$.
   b. The coupon should be printed at $6 = 12 - 4 \cdot (-3/-2)$.

CHAPTER 9

Bundling and Intrafirm Pricing

Chapter Profile

Bundling is a way for firms to increase profits by selling two or more goods as if they were one. For the bundling technique to maximize profits, the reservation price of the goods of different consumer types must be negatively correlated (that is, some customers put a higher value on one of the goods, and other customers put a higher value on the other good), and price discrimination among customers must be difficult. **Pure bundling** is selling goods only in bundles. **Mixed bundling** allows for selling goods separately as well. The manager will choose the best solution that is profit maximizing, and it may be by separate pricing, pure bundling, or mixed bundling.

Many large firms are decentralized, which may require one division of the firm to sell its product to another division of the firm. To maximize the firm's overall profit, it is important that the price at which this transfer takes place is set properly. This price is called the **transfer price**. If there is no market outside of the firm for the transferred product, the transfer price should equal the marginal production cost at the optimal output. If there is a perfectly competitive market for the transferred product outside the firm, the transfer price should equal the price of this product in that market. Transfer pricing is also very important in international trade, where firms may encounter costly tax issues resulting from the valuation of shipments of goods from a plant in one nation to a plant in another nation.

Questions

Completion

1. Bundling is a form of price discrimination that is useful to companies in maximizing profits when consumers have reservation prices for two types of products that are _____ related.

2. Transfer pricing involves pricing within _____ of a firm.

3. To successfully engage in tying, a firm must have significant market _____.

4. Offering bundle pricing and separate pricing at the same time is known as _____ bundling.

5. Bundling can increase revenue when price discrimination is _____.

True or False

       _____   1.   Tying refers to a firm selling a product that requires the consumption of a substitute product as well.

       _____   2.   Bundling can enable a firm to emulate perfect price discrimination when it is otherwise difficult or illegal.

       _____   3.   Finding the optimal bundle is a trial and error procedure.

       _____   4.   Bundling is best used when goods are substitutes.

       _____   5.   Transfer pricing is used to shift profits among divisions to minimize tax liability.

Multiple Choice

1. Goods and services are considered bundled when:

    a.   they are sold together in defined quantities
    b.   they are sold separately but advertised together
    c.   they are sold separately but displayed together
    d.   they are sold together but can be mixed and matched by the store owner
    e.   they are sold separately but wrapped together by the store owner

2. In a perfectly competitive situation, transfer pricing:

    a.   forces the firm to price its internal transfers at an unfair price
    b.   makes the firm lose money on internal transfers
    c.   encourages managers to price internal transfers at artificially high rates
    d.   reduces the incentive for managers to act independently
    e.   encourages managers to sell or buy products on the open market

3. If there is no market outside the firm for the transferred product, the transfer price should:

    a.   equal the average cost of the transferred product at the optimal output
    b.   equal the average variable cost of the transferred product at the optimal output
    c.   equal the demand for the transferred product at the optimal output
    d.   equal the marginal revenue for the transferred product at the optimal output
    e.   equal the marginal production cost of the transferred product at the optimal output

4. Tying is a form of bundling that involves:

    a.   contractual arrangements requiring the sale of complementary products from the firm selling the main product
    b.   two firms selling complementary products to the same customer
    c.   different customers buying the same product
    d.   producing two similar products
    e.   combining the cost of production of different products

5. A vertically integrated firm may use transfer pricing to:

    a.   simulate a market situation when none really exists
    b.   optimally profit-maximize decisions by managers among internal firm units

c. reduce taxes by shifting profits among divisions in different political jurisdictions
d. all of the above
e. none of the above

Problems

1. Bob and Ron's Stereo still sells televisions and separate DVD players. The company has estimated the demand for these items and determined that there are three consumer types (A, B, and C) of equal number (assume one for simplicity) that have the following reservation prices for the two products. Bob and Ron's cost for a unit of each item is $9.

	DVD player	TV
A	12	28
B	4	29
C	10	30

Any consumer's reservation price for a bundle of one DVD player and one TV would be the sum of the reservation prices for each item. Consumers will demand (at most) one DVD player and one TV, e.g., a consumer would never buy a DVD player *and* a bundle or would never buy 2 TVs.

a. If Bob and Ron's Stereo only considered pricing each item separately, pricing a pure bundle, or pricing a mixed bundle, what price(s) would it charge and what would its profit be?

Bob and Ron's price(s) would be: _____

Bob and Ron's profit would be: _____

b. If Bob and Ron's Stereo were able to perfectly price discriminate, how much would its profit increase over its optimal profit in part a?

Bob and Ron's profit would increase by: _____

2. The Hayes Company is composed of a marketing division and a production division. The production division produces a raw material that it transfers to the marketing division. There is an external market for this raw material; the price in this market (which is perfectly competitive) is $18 per pound. The production division's average cost of production is $22 per pound.

a. The vice president of production argues that the transfer price for this raw material should be $22. Otherwise his division cannot cover its costs. Is he correct? Why or why not?

b. The vice president of marketing argues that the transfer price should be $18. Otherwise her division is paying more than it needs to. Is she correct? Why or why not?

3. The XYZ television network is a startup network with only two shows (the *Donald Trumpet* cooking show and the *Martha Stowit* real estate show). It is in the process of putting together its advertising prices for the coming season.

It estimates that there are three classes of advertisers (A, B, and C), and there are an equal number of advertisers in each class (call it one in each class for simplicity). Price discrimination is not allowed. For example, every advertiser will pay the same rate to advertise on the Trumpet show. Likewise, every advertiser will pay the same rate to advertise on the *Stowit* show (but not necessarily the same rate as for the *Trumpet* show). Should XYZ decide to bundle the two shows together for advertising purposes, every advertiser would pay the same price for the bundle. The rates cover the whole season. Clearly, an advertiser would not purchase advertising for one show twice, nor would an advertiser purchase the advertising bundle and advertising on a single show.

The table below represents XYZ's estimate of the reservation prices for a season of advertising of the advertisers for each show and for the bundle. It costs XYZ $3 to provide the advertising services to each advertiser for each show for the season and $6 to provide the advertising bundle for the season.

Advertiser	Trumpet	Stowit	Bundle of both shows
A	15	10	25
B	9	11	20
C	2	19	21

What are XYZ's profits if it sells advertising for each show separately, as a pure bundle, or as a mixed bundle?

a. The maximum profit and prices if XYZ prices separately are: _____
b. The maximum profit and price if XYZ pure bundles are: _____
c. The maximum profit and prices if XYZ mixed bundles are: _____

4. Macrohard produces two products to be used on computers. The first is a word processing program called English, and the second is a spreadsheet program called Numbers. Macrohard has segmented its customer base into three categories and estimated the reservation price for each customer type for each of its two products. The reservation price for a bundle of the two products is the sum of the reservation prices for each product. Three types of customers exist: A, the novelist, who values the word processing more than the spreadsheet; C, the accountant, who values the spreadsheet more than the word processing; and B, the generalist, who values both products equally. There are an equal number of each customer type (say one of each). Each consumer wants no more than one of each product (e.g., no one wants two English programs; no one would buy a bundle of the two programs and then a Numbers program). The table below sets out the customers' reservation prices for the products.

Customer	English	Numbers
A	$15	$12
B	$14	$14
C	$9	$13

a. Macrohard is contemplating selling each product separately, as a pure bundle, or as a mixed bundle. Given that it costs $4 to produce each product, what pricing strategy maximizes Macrohard's profits?
b. Macrohard should (price separately, pure bundle, or mixed bundle)? With prices of?
c. This pricing policy is _____ better than the second best pricing policy.

Answers

Completion
1. inversely   2. divisions   3. power   4. mixed   5. impossible

True or False
1. False   2. True   3. True   4. False   5. True

Multiple Choice
1. a   2. e   3. e   4. e   5. d

Problems

1. a. Consider pricing separately:

P_{DVD}	AC_{DVD}	$\Pi/Unit_{DVD}$	#DVDs	Π_{DVD}
12	9	3	1	3 ← Best
4	9	−5	3	−15
10	9	1	2	2

P_{TV}	AC_{TV}	$\Pi/Unit_{TV}$	#TVs	Π_{TV}
28	9	19	3	57 ← Best
29	9	20	2	40
30	9	21	1	21

Thus, the best price separately is $P_{DVD} = \$12$ and $P_{TV} = \$28$, yielding a profit of $3 + 57 = \$60$.

Consider a pure bundle:

P_{bun}	AC_{bun}	$\Pi/Unit_{bun}$	#Bundles	Π_{bun}
$40	18	22	2	44
$33	18	15	3	45 ← Best

Thus, the best pure bundle price is $P_{bun} = \$33$ yielding a profit of $45.

Consider a mixed bundle:

P_{bun}	AC_{bun}	$\Pi/Unit_{bun}$	#Bundles	Π_{bun}
39⁻	18	21⁻	2 (A&C)	42⁻

P_{TV}	AC_{TV}	$\Pi/Unit_{TV}$	#TVs	Π_{TV}
29	9	20	1(B)	20

Thus, the best mixed bundle is $P_{bun} = \$39$ and $P_{TV} = 29$ and not offering DVDs separately, which would yield a profit of $42^- + 20 = \$62^-$. Therefore, this is the most profitable pricing policy.

b. If Bob and Ron's Stereo could perfectly price discriminate, it would sell DVDs to consumers A and C for $12 and $10, respectively, bringing in $22 in revenue, and it would sell TVs to A, B, and C for $28, $29, and $30, respectively, for revenues of $87. This gives total revenues of $22 + $87 = $109. Since it sold five items at a cost of $9 per item, its total costs are $5 \times \$9 = \$45$. Its profit if it perfectly price discriminates is thus

$109 - 45 = \$64$. This is $64 - 62^{--} = 2^{++}$ better than following the best mixed bundling strategy.

Note that Bob and Ron's Stereo would not perfectly price discriminate on the pure bundles (at least not to consumer B—who will not pay the cost of a DVD). If it did, it would charge $40, $33, and $40, respectively, to A, B, and C for total revenue of $113. Since it would sell six items, its cost is $9 \times 6 = \$54$, and profit would only be $113 - 54 = \$59$.

2. a. No, the transfer price should be $18.
   b. Yes.

3. a. Consider pricing separately:

$P_{Trumpet}$	Unit cost$_{Trumpet}$	Profit/Unit$_{Trumpet}$	#Units$_{Trumpet}$	Profit$_{Trumpet}$
15	3	12	1	12 ← Best
9	3	6	2	12 ← Best
2	3	−1	3	−3

P_{Stowit}	Unit cost$_{Stowit}$	Profit/Unit$_{Stowit}$	#Units$_{Stowit}$	Profit$_{Stowit}$
10	3	7	3	21 ← Best
11	3	8	2	16
19	3	16	1	26

So the best price separately prices are $P_{Trumpet} = \$15$ or $P_{Trumpet} = \$9$ and $P_{Stowit} = \$10$, which yields a profit of $12 + 21 = \$33$.

   b. Consider pure bundling:

P_{bundle}	Unit cost$_{bundle}$	Profit/Bundle	#Bundles	Profit$_{bundle}$
25	6	19	1	19
20	6	14	3	42 ← Best
21	6	15	2	30

So, the best pure bundle price is $P_{bundle} = \$20$, which yields a profit of $42.

   c. Consider mixed bundling:

P_{bundle}	Unit cost$_{bundle}$	Profit/Bundle	#Bundles	Profit$_{bundle}$
20	6	14	2 (A&B)	28

P_{Stowit}	Unit cost$_{Stowit}$	Profit/Unit$_{Stowit}$	#Units$_{Stowit}$	Profit$_{Stowit}$
18^-	3	15^-	1(C)	15^-

The best mixed bundling prices are $P_{bundle} = \$20$, $P_{Stowit} = \$18^-$, and don't offer Trumpet separately, which yields a profit of $28 + 15^- = \$43^-$.

4. a. Consider pricing separately:

P_E	C_E	$\Pi/Unit_E$	#Units$_E$	Π_E	P_N	C_N	$\Pi/Unit_N$	#Units$_N$	Π_N
15	4	11	1	11	12	4	8	3	24 ← Best
14	4	10	2	20 ← Best	14	4	10	1	10
9	4	5	3	15	13	4	9	2	18

Thus, the best price separately policy is to price the English product at $14 and make $20, and price the Numbers product at $12 and make $24 for a total profit of $20 + 24 = $44.

Consider a pure bundle:

P_{bun}	C_{bun}	Π/Bundle	#Bundles	Π_{bun}
27	8	19	2	38
28	8	20	1	20
22	8	14	3	42 ← Best

Thus, the best bundle price is $22 for a total profit of $42.

Consider a mixed bundle:

P_{bun}	C_{bun}	Π/Bundle	#Bundles	Π_{bun}
27^-	8	19^-	2 (A&B)	38^-

P_N	C_N	Π/Unit$_N$	#Units$_N$	Π_N
13	4	9	1 (C)	9

b. Thus, the best mixed bundle is to sell the bundle at 27^- to A and B for a profit of 38^- and sell Numbers for $13 to C for a profit of $9, for a total profit of $38^- + 9 = 47^-. Note that B will buy the bundle because they receive a consumer surplus of $28 − 27^- = 1^+ by doing so. If B bought just Numbers for 13, they would only receive a consumer surplus of $14 − 13 = $1.

c. Thus, the best pricing strategy is to mixed bundle with the bundle at 27^- to A and B for a profit of 38^- and sell Numbers for $13 to C for a profit of $9, for a total profit of $38^- + 9 = 47^-. The next best pricing strategy is to price separately with English priced at $14 for a profit of $20 and Numbers priced at $12 for a profit of $24, yielding a total profit of $44. The best pricing strategy is $47^- − 44 = 3^- better than the second best strategy.

CASE THREE

Déjà vu: The Internet and Past Innovations
Michael Totty

You hear it all the time: The Internet is the railroad of the 21st century. That is, unless it's the radio. Or maybe the telegraph. Or perhaps the printing press.

These comparisons are always made, but are they valid? Are the inventions of the past really similar to the Net of today? More important, can we learn anything about the present—and future—of the Internet by looking at what happened with previous technology revolutions?

Perhaps, but if nothing else, the exercise helps put our well-hyped era into perspective. Here's a look at four technologies that changed the world and how they parallel—and differ from—the development so far of the Internet.

THE PRINTING PRESS
(Created 1450s)

The birth of the printing press in the 15th century marked the first information revolution. It produced the kind of social and cultural changes only dreamed of by promoters of the Internet.

It may not have launched the Renaissance, but it certainly guaranteed that the movement wouldn't evaporate like earlier revivals of classical writings. It spread the works of Martin Luther and John Calvin, effectively bringing about the Protestant Reformation. And it made possible the extensive exchange of scientific information, including maps and astronomical charts, laying the foundation for modern science. It isn't too much of a stretch to say that printing helped create the modern world.

The technology came together in the early 1450s in the workshop of Johannes Gutenberg, a German craftsman, whose printed Bible was among the first works created using the new medium. Herr Gutenberg, who saw a business opportunity in the growing demand for books, brought together a handful of existing technologies to change the way we communicate through printed words.

Printing quickly spread throughout Europe—within 15 years of Gutenberg's death in 1468 printing presses were established in every European country—mainly by craftsman-entrepreneurs who found a market in printing books, circulars and sermons.

Parallels:

The printing press loosened the grip on information held by the Church in the

---

Renaissance, much as the Internet has created an alternative to the mass-media companies today, allowing individuals to bypass the traditional information outlets to reach bigger audiences. Martin Luther, meet Matt Drudge.

In the Internet's early days, it wasn't uncommon to hear people say they couldn't imagine reading a newspaper online, or communicating with loved ones by e-mail. Printed books encountered similar resistance among some aristocratic collectors, who dominated the book-buying public. Duke Federigo de Urbino, for instance, is reported to have said that in his library, "all books were superlatively good and written with a pen; had there been one printed book, it would have been ashamed in such company." Cost and convenience eventually meant the new books would win out with less picky buyers.

If sharing digital copies over the Internet poses a threat to copyrighted works, you can thank the rise of printing for the very notion of "copyright." "Printing forced legal definition of what belonged in the public domain," writes historian Elizabeth Eisenstein in "The Printing Revolution in Early Modern Europe." "The terms plagiarism and copyright did not exist for the minstrel. It was only after printing that they began to hold significance for the author."

Differences:

The pioneers of the printing press didn't have to struggle to find a business model— printing from the start was a successful commercial enterprise. (Still, Gutenberg himself was more like today's dot-com pioneers: After launching his press with a loan from a local lawyer, Johann Fust, Gutenberg was unable to repay the debt. Fust foreclosed on Gutenberg's nascent operation and turned it over to an employee and future son-in-law, Peter Schoeffer. Schoeffer turned it into a thriving business.)

Another difference: Printing was and is the province of skilled artisans and requires costly equipment. Publishing over the Internet requires virtually no special skills or equipment beyond a personal computer, effectively putting a printing press on every desk or dinner table.

Lessons:

The Internet probably won't prove to be as revolutionary as printing: While books, pamphlets and other information sources were a relatively rare commodity in 15th-century Europe, we already live in an age awash with information. Still, just as with the printing press, the speed with which information can be exchanged around the globe via the Net is already transforming fields from science to public opinion. One example: Thanks to the Net, researchers all over the world can get access to emerging information about the human genome, speeding understanding of how it works.

And it's still early: Even though printing spread rapidly, it took more than 100 years for some of the big social and cultural effects to appear.

THE TELEGRAPH (Created 1830s)

The telegraph was the first telecommunications network, the first to erase the old physical limits of time and distance. British journalist Tom Standage didn't really have to stretch much when, in a 1998 history, he called the telegraph "The Victorian Internet."

It transformed the news business, making it possible for newspapers to publish reports of distant events the next day— sometimes within hours. (The second message on the first commercial telegraph line between Washington and Baltimore, after "What hath God wrought?" was "Have you any news?") It helped create the modern stock market, and took financial markets and businesses global. It also led directly to the telephone, the radio and electric power.

Invented nearly simultaneously in 1837 by William Cooke and Charles Wheatstone in England and by Samuel F. B. Morse in the U.S., the electrical telegraph replaced "optical" telegraphy, which carried messages over long distances by an elaborate set of visual signals.

Initially, the telegraph was seen as a novelty, but not as anything that had practical uses. Still, it took only eight years from its invention until the launch of the first commercial telegraph line. By 1850, there were 12,000 miles of telegraph lines in the U.S. By 1858, the trans-Atlantic cable linked Europe and the U.S.

Parallels:

Like the Internet, the telegraph inspired an outpouring of enthusiasm and hype about the promise of the new medium, especially with the laying of the trans-Atlantic cable. Books explaining its operation were rushed into print, and dot-com-style hyperbole filled the papers. "It is impossible that old prejudices and hostilities should longer exist, while such an instrument has been created for an exchange of thought between all the nations of the earth," wrote the authors of one contemporary history of the telegraph.

Success bred congestion, much like the way America Online's system was overwhelmed by the influx of new customers in the mid-1990s. So many messages flooded telegraph offices in the 1850s that delays inevitably ensued. To ease the bottleneck between the main London telegraph office and the stock exchange, the local telegraph office came up with a nonelectric solution— a system of pneumatic tubes to carry handwritten messages between the exchange and the main office. The solution was so successful that pneumatic-tube networks spread throughout London and were adopted in other cities as well.

Like the shorthand used by online teens to send instant messages between friends, telegraph operators created their own abbreviations for keeping telegraph messages short: "G M" for good morning, for instance, or "S F D" for stop for dinner. Businesses adopted codes for another reason: to hold down the high cost of telegraph messages, especially going overseas. Thick commercial books were printed to hold the intricate codes. In one, Mr. Standage writes, the British Department of Agriculture in India used the word "envelope" to mean "great swarms of locusts have appeared and ravaged the crops."

There also grew up a subculture of telegraph operators. They weren't called nerds or geeks, but they were separated from their contemporaries by their mastery of the telegraphic code. Transcontinental friendships grew up, and long-distance romances bloomed.

Another striking similarity with the Internet was the supposed effect telegraphs would have on newspapers. "The telegraph may not affect magazine literature," said New York Herald Editor James Gordon Bennett, "but the mere newspapers must submit to destiny and go out of existence." Instead, the telegraph turned out to be a godsend for newspapers, making news gathering faster and easier.

Finally, what is it about France: It pioneers a technology and then is slow to adopt its successor. The optical telegraph was developed in France and sent its first message in 1791, but by 1852 it had half the electrical telegraph miles of Prussia. Likewise, France's Minitel network was an early success story as an online data service, and its aficionados have kept it thriving long after other countries have adopted the Internet.

Differences:

Commercial adoption of the telegraph happened much more quickly than it did with the Internet. It was more than 25 years from the birth of the Internet until Amazon.com sold its first book in 1995. By contrast, the first commercial telegraph line in the U.S.,

Morse's Washington-to-Baltimore line, was launched within eight years of the telegraph's invention.

The telegraph remained in the hands of professionals and skilled hobbyists and never became a mass-market phenomenon, like the radio, telephone and the Internet. What's more, telegraph operations remained or quickly became business or government monopolies.

And, unlike the Internet, the telegraph never overcame its serious bandwidth shortage. So it remained a medium of short messages, especially in international communications, where the costs were often extremely high.

Lessons:

Information wants to be free, unless you have to pay someone to deliver it. Both the printing press and the telegraph were commercial successes almost from the start because they acted as bottlenecks—anyone who wanted a book printed or a message sent had to go through someone with a press or a telegraph line, and both were expensive enterprises to launch. With the Internet, it costs almost nothing to send a newspaper or a book, but it's still costly to produce them. If that difference is significant, it may be bad news for anyone wanting to make a lot of money sending information over the Internet.

RAILROADS (Created 1820s)

The Internet is mainly a communications medium, so it's easy to see the comparisons with the printing press and the telegraph. But why do many commentators liken it to the 19th-century railroads?

Because, like the Internet, the railroads linked markets and individuals faster than anything before, and because, especially in Britain, they experienced an investment mania and subsequent bust—long before the industry saw its heyday. It's an upbeat story for depressing times.

The economic, social and political effects of railroads were certainly large. They dramatically lowered the cost of shipping goods and, in the process, the cost of the goods themselves. Business historians credit railroads with creating a national economy in the U.S. out of disjointed local and regional markets. Also, because they were among the first large-scale enterprises with far-flung operations, railroads contributed to the creation of modern management and accounting practices. The immense wealth and power concentrated by the railroads eventually led to a popular backlash: They can be credited with helping create the 19th-century Progressive movement and led to the formation of the Interstate Commerce Commission, the first federal regulatory agency.

The first commercial railroad set off in 1825 between the coal town of Darlington and the river port of Stockton in northern England (the success of the line helped drop the portside price of coal to 12 shillings a ton from 18 shillings), and the first line in the U.S. opened five years later.

This kicked off a frenzy of railroad construction and a frenzy among investors. The British "railway mania" of the 1840s attracted investors from all stations of life, and the subsequent bust in 1847 "reached every hearth," wrote John Francis, a contemporary historian, as cited in an article by W. Brian Arthur, an economist at the Santa Fe Institute in New Mexico. "Entire families were ruined."

Yet railroads bounced back, doubling their mileage and quadrupling the number of passengers carried by the 1870s, and tripling their revenue in just five years after the bust. In the U.S., the 1860s saw the construction of the transcontinental railroad, and world-wide the rails dominated land transportation until the rise of the automobile.

Parallels:

While the Internet brought day traders and online investing in its wake, the railroads also transformed 19th-century stock markets in the U.S. and Britain. Historian John Steele Gordon writes that railroad securities contributed to the rapid growth of trading on the New York Stock Exchange in the 1850s; at the time, two-thirds of the issues were railroad stocks and bonds.

The early days of rail came with a stock bubble in Britain, where financial markets were more developed than in the U.S. Stock ownership rose dramatically in Britain during the 1840s as it was going through its railroad mania. For those who couldn't afford stock, shares were divvied up into fractional shares, called scrip, which were sold to tailors and servants. "There was a frenzy of speculation," says Mr. Arthur, the economist.

The railroad also transformed retailing, creating a national market for giant retailers. Sears Roebuck was the Amazon.com of its day, making goods available nationwide at a cheaper price than they could be purchased locally. Its catalogs offered a seemingly impossible abundance of merchandise.

Differences:

Even more than with telegraphs and printing presses, railroads required huge upfront investments, so from the start they were controlled by those who could muster the financial and operational resources to start and run them—they were never the creation of two guys in a garage. Railroad operators could amass great wealth, and great power, something no one has been able to do with the Internet.

Lessons:

Technology survives mania. The lesson most commentators draw from all this is that the best days of the Internet are still ahead. "After the crash, the technology most people think is ruined goes on to achieve a golden age," says Mr. Arthur. "The transformative period of the Internet is still ahead of us."

Another conclusion from some historians: It largely won't be the Internet pioneers who benefit financially. Mr. Gordon, the historian, notes that the ones who got really rich with railroads were those people, such as Cornelius Vanderbilt, who sat on the sidelines during the initial boom. Still, Mr. Gordon cautions, "We're really so much at the very beginning of this. [The commercial Internet] is only seven years old. We're still like the railroad in the 1830s."

RADIO (Created 1906)

Radio reinvented the notion of mass culture, bringing together numbers of listeners unmatched in history. During its heyday in the 1930s, 30 million to 50 million listeners tuned into the most popular program every week. Contrast that with what is considered to be the best-selling fiction book of all time, "The Valley of the Dolls," which has sold more than 30 million copies since it was published in 1966.

The first wireless signals were sent by Guglielmo Marconi in 1895, and the technology was used for sending telegraph messages to places—primarily offshore ships — not connected by wires. But it was another decade before the first radio broadcast, and 15 years after that, before the first radio station—KDKA in Pittsburgh—began broadcasting regular programs.

Radio rapidly took off from there, as consumers rushed to buy sets for listening to the broadcasts, and stations appeared to fill the airwaves. The National Broadcasting Corp. put together the first radio network, while Radio Corp. of America became the darling of investors, leading the booming stock market of the 1920s.

Parallels:

The first modern mass medium, radio is the technology that most closely traced the development arc followed by the Internet: early adoption by government, business and dedicated hobbyists, followed by rapid commercialization, popular frenzy, investment mania, speculative bubble and crash—all before really hitting its stride. (For the Internet, the last stage remains to be seen.)

Just as with the Internet, early radio users were hobbyists, and these "radio boys" fit a familiar profile: Most were young, middle-class and overwhelmingly male. They were content to spend long hours, often late into the night, scanning the airwaves for distant signals and sending out their own messages, usually on sets they built from scrounged parts. They dominated the radio waves until the military took charge of the medium in World War I.

Skeptics, while recognizing the marvel of radio communications, questioned its commercial potential. The criticism was, "How could someone make money by conveying messages that all could hear?" writes Debora L. Spar, a professor of international business at the Harvard Business School, in her book *Ruling the Waves*.

Yet, as in the dot-com stock bubble, skepticism quickly morphed into irrational exuberance. RCA stock rose from $85 in early 1928 to over $200 by June, $400 by November and reached $500 by the summer of 1929. (It then split 5-for-1.) At that time, a $10,000 investment in 1921 was worth over $1 million. After the market crash, RCA fell to lower than $20 and that investment was worth $20,000.

Radio was the Napster of its day, accused of ripping off composers and programmers by giving listeners free music. As more and more stations relied on recorded music for their programming, the American Society of Composers, Authors and Publishers complained that the broadcasts were depriving its members of royalties. Backed by court rulings, the group eventually forced stations to pay an annual license fee to broadcast any ASCAP-controlled music.

Differences:

In the U.S., the federal government generally has limited its meddling in the Internet to mediating copyright disputes and trying to block children's access to pornography. Otherwise, it has pretty much left cyberspace alone.

Congestion in the airwaves made radio different. In 1912 Congress passed the first radio act, requiring all operators to be licensees and giving priority to emergency messages. A tougher law was adopted in 1927 to deal with the chaos of broadcasters' interfering with other stations' signals unleashed by the 1920s radio boom. The 1927 law created the Federal Radio Commission (later the Federal Communications Commission) and gave Washington control over the airwaves; stations could use the broadcast spectrum, but they didn't own it. In radio, unlike the Internet, government could pick winners and losers, and government could choose who could operate and who couldn't.

Lessons:

The radio experience provides a cautionary note for the online startups that hope to profit by playing niche music on the Web. Initially, dozens of small, largely amateur radio stations provided quirky, locally produced programs to serve their communities. But commercial and other pressures either drove them out of business or forced them into the arms of the growing radio networks, such as NBC.

The networks were able to deliver the most popular programs via affiliates all over the country, and a lot of amateurish local programming couldn't compete. Adding to the problems of the smaller stations were the license fees stations had to pay to ASCAP. This hit the smaller amateur-run stations the hardest, Harvard's Ms. Spar notes, forcing many of them to seek corporate sponsorships or go out of business. Now that record labels have succeeded in forcing Internet radio stations to pay a license fee for the use of their music, look for a similar shakeout in online radio.

Those who predict the best days of the Internet are still ahead can take consolation in what happened to radio after the '29 crash wiped out the fortune of many of radio's pioneers. But that may be little comfort to investors. RCA stock didn't return to its pre-crash levels until 1954—in the midst of an investor frenzy over television.

Will government regulation come to the Internet the way it eventually came to dominate the radio, and later television, industries? On the one hand, the Net is too sprawling and decentralized for Washington to seize control the way it did with the airwaves, nor does it face the kinds of congestion that forced government action.

But if history is any guide, look for an increasing role for government in cyberspace. There are moves afoot to end the generally tax-free status of most e-commerce. Copyright holders are increasingly holding sway in their battle to enforce property rights online. And consumers are demanding protection for their privacy rights.

"We are going to move into a phase of increasing regulation," Ms. Spar says. While it won't be the same kind of strict control seen with radio, she says, "it will be more or less the same kind of regulatory structure we've seen in every other new technology, which also looked like it couldn't be regulated when it first came around."

Questions

1. Note and discuss the time span between each invention and its diffusion and acceptance in business. Have modern communications made it faster?

2. Discuss the role of the telegraph in helping to create the modern stock market. Note two things: first, that each new innovation is a building block for future technologies; and second, that many of the innovations described in this case study became essential parts of the infrastructure that supported further economic growth.

3. Initially, many of the communications technologies of the past required little money to enter the industry and compete. The Internet has also opened up access to global communications at very small startup costs. From the history of past communications technologies, do you expect the startup costs of Internet businesses to increase or decrease in the future? Why?

Part Six

THE STRATEGIC WORLD OF MANAGERS

CHAPTER 10

Oligopoly

Chapter Profile

Oligopoly is characterized by a small number of firms and a great deal of interdependence, actual and perceived, among them. A good example of an oligopoly is the American oil industry, where a small number of firms account for the bulk of the industry's capacity.

Oligopolistic industries, like others, tend to pass through a number of phases—introduction, growth, maturity, and decline. As an industry goes through these phases, the nature of firm behavior often shifts. During the early stages, there often is considerable uncertainty regarding the industry's technology and concerning which markets will open up soonest. During the maturity phase, there frequently is a tendency for firms to attack the market shares of their rivals. In decline, there may be a tendency to get cash out of the firm as quickly as possible, but this may not be the best policy.

There is no single model of oligopoly. Instead, there are many models, depending on the circumstances. Conditions in oligopolistic industries tend to promote collusion, since the number of firms is small and firms recognize their interdependence. The advantages to be derived by the firms from collusion seem obvious: increased profits, decreased uncertainty, and a better opportunity to control the entry of new firms. However, collusive arrangements are often hard to maintain, since once a collusive agreement is made, any of the firms can increase its profits by "cheating" on the agreement.

A model of oligopolistic behavior is based on the supposition that one of the firms in the industry is a **price leader**, because it is a dominant firm. The Cournot scenario illustrates how under these circumstances this firm should set its price to maximize its profits. Another model of the rivalry and reactions among competitors in an oligopolistic industry focuses on production capacity decisions (the Stackelberg model). The kinked-demand curve model illustrates why prices in an oligopolistic industry are "sticky" and tend not to change very often.

Statistical studies based on data pertaining to hundreds of firms indicate that (1) the single most important factor influencing a business unit's profitability is the quality of its products and services, relative to those of rivals, and (2) market share and profitability are strongly related.

Questions

Completion

1. All firms in an industry have marginal costs equal to $10 per unit of output. If they combine to form a cartel, the cartel's marginal cost (will, will not) _____ be $10 per unit of output. If the cartel maximizes profit, its marginal revenue will be (greater than, smaller than, equal to) _____ $10 per unit. Its price will be (greater than, smaller than, equal to) _____ $10 per unit.

2. Under oligopoly, each firm is aware that its actions are likely to elicit _____ in the policies of its competitors.

3. A good example of oligopoly in the United States is the _____ industry.

4. Excess _____ can be used to forestall and resist entry.

5. According to PIMS data, the most important single factor influencing a business unit's profitability is the _____ of its products and services relative to those of rivals.

6. The Cournot model assumes that each firm thinks that the other will hold its output constant at _____.

True or False

_____ 1. Collusion is often difficult to achieve and maintain because an oligopoly contains an unwieldy number of firms, or because the product is quite heterogeneous.

_____ 2. If a perfectly competitive industry is operating along the elastic portion of its demand curve, there is no point in trying to cartelize the industry.

_____ 3. Because a cartel maximizes profit, there is no incentive for a member to violate the rules of the cartel.

_____ 4. Cartels have been common and legally acceptable in Europe.

_____ 5. Cartels tend to be unstable because the demand curve facing a "cheater" is highly inelastic.

_____ 6. According to the dominant-firm model, the dominant firm allows the smaller firms to sell all they want at the price it sets.

_____ 7. Whether or not an industry remains oligopolistic in the face of relatively easy entry depends on the size of the market for the product relative to the optimal size of the firm.

_____ 8. Firms that participate under a collusive agreement can increase their individual profitability by increasing their production.

_____ 9. Consumer surplus is lower in an oligopolistic market than in a perfectly competitive market.

_____ 10. If all firms in an industry charge the same price for their product, that is conclusive evidence of collusive behavior.

Multiple Choice

1. A firm may be able to deter entry into its market by:

    a. building excess production capacity
    b. gaining a reputation for "irrational" resistance to entry
    c. threatening to resist even though potential entrants believe that it is not in this firm's interest to resist
    d. only a and b
    e. all of the above

2. If D is the industry demand curve and marginal cost equals $2, the price that maximizes a cartel's profits is:

    a. $12
    b. $14
    c. $16
    d. $2
    e. none of the above

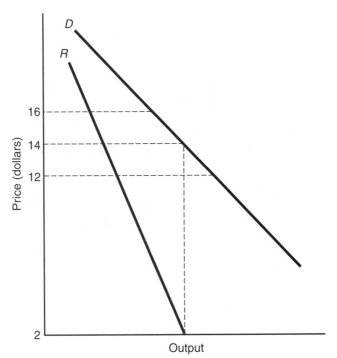

3. In the previous question, the R curve is:

    a. the marginal revenue curve
    b. the marginal cost curve
    c. the reaction curve
    d. all of the above
    e. none of the above

4. In the dominant-firm model, the dominant firm finds the demand curve for its output by:

   a. using the unadjusted industry demand curve
   b. adding up the small firms' demand curves
   c. subtracting the small firms' supply from the industry demand curve
   d. all of the above
   e. none of the above

Problems

1. During the 1960s and 1970s, the major U.S. automobile manufacturers were not very enthusiastic about producing small cars, owing in part to the fact that they made a larger profit on a larger car than a smaller one. But the explosion of gasoline prices and the press of foreign competition during the 1970s led the American producers to introduce new lines of smaller, fuel-efficient cars in the fall of 1980. The prices at which they and their Japanese competitors were offered were as follows:

Chevrolet Citation	$6,337	Subaru wagon	$5,612
GM "J" cars	6,300	Datsun 310	5,439
Ford Escort	6,009	Subaru hatchback	5,212
Dodge Omni	5,713	Mazda GLC	4,755

   a. According to some observers, "Detroit…priced these cars relatively high to replenish its depleted coffers as soon as possible." Is this necessarily the effect of charging relatively high prices?

   b. Some auto executives stated that the U.S. demand for smaller cars would be so great in the early 1980s that Detroit would be able to sell all such cars that it could produce. What implicit assumptions were they making?

2. There are ten identical producers of spring water. Each of these firms has zero costs of production, so long as it produces less than (or equal to) 10 gallons of water per hour. It is impossible for each firm to produce more than 10 gallons per hour. Suppose the market demand curve for this water is as follows:

Price (dollars per gallon)	Number of gallons demanded per hour	Price (dollars per gallon)	Number of gallons demanded per hour
11	0	5	60
10	10	4	70
9	20	3	80
8	30	2	90
7	40	1	100
6	50	½	105

   a. If the firms take the price of water as given (as in the case of perfect competition), what will be the price and output of each firm?

   b. If the firms form a completely effective cartel, what will be the price and output of each firm?

   c. How much money will each firm be willing to pay to achieve and enforce the collusive agreement described in part b?

   d. Suppose that one of the firms secretly breaks the terms of the agreement and shades price. What effect will this have on its profits?

3. The Aloha Company and the Crowe Corporation are producers of a product whose marginal cost equals $2. The marginal revenue curve for their combined output is

$$MR = 10 - 2Q$$

where MR is marginal revenue (in dollars), and Q is the number of units of output sold by both together per hour. If the two producers decide to collude and share the monopoly profits, how much will be their combined output? Why?

4. A cartel is formed by three firms. Their total cost functions are as follows:

Total cost (dollars)

Units of output	Firm A	Firm B	Firm C
0	20	25	15
1	25	35	22
2	35	50	32
3	50	80	47
4	80	120	77
5	120	160	117

If the cartel decides to produce 11 units of output, how should the output be distributed among the three firms if they want to minimize cost?

5. In its annual report, Aluminium, Ltd., of Canada once noted, "World stocks of aluminum are not excessively large. They are in firm hands and do not weigh unduly upon the world market." What did it mean by "firm hands"? Do you think this phenomenon was at all related to the firmness of world aluminum prices during the relevant period? Under perfect competition, do you think aluminum prices would remain fairly constant in the face of sharp reductions in sales?

6. U.S. Steel (now USX) often was regarded as the price leader in steel, as was Alcoa in virgin aluminum, American Viscose in rayon, and DuPont in nylon and polyester fibers. What characteristics tend to distinguish price leaders from other firms? If you had to predict which of a number of firms in an industry was the price leader, what variables would you use to make the forecast?

7. According to the Federal Trade Commission, there was collusion among the leading bakers and food outlets in the state of Washington in the late 1950s and early 1960s. Prior to the conspiracy, bread prices in Seattle were about equal to the U.S. average. During the period of the conspiracy, bread prices in Seattle were 15 to 20 percent above the U.S. average. Is this consistent with the theory of collusive behavior? Why do you think bread prices in Seattle were not double or triple the U.S. average during the conspiracy?

Answers

Completion
1. will, equal to, greater than   2. changes   3. steel (among many others)
4. capacity   5. quality   6. its existing level

True or False

1. True   2. False   3. False   4. True   5. False   6. True   7. True   8. True
9. True   10. False

Multiple Choice

1. d   2. b   3. a   4. c

Problems

1. a. No. If a firm charges relatively high prices, it may sell relatively few units of
its product, the result being that its profits may be lower than they would be
if its price were somewhat lower.

   b. They were assuming that U.S. consumers would not buy imported smaller
cars (instead of U.S. smaller cars) in such numbers that Detroit would be
unable to sell all it could produce.

2. a. The industry supply curve would be as follows. This is the horizontal sum
of the firm's marginal cost curves. Since this supply curve intersects the
demand curve at a price of $1, this is the equilibrium price. Since the supply
and demand curves intersect at an output of 100 gallons, this is the industry
output. Each firm produces one-tenth of this output, or 10 gallons. The
industry supply curve is

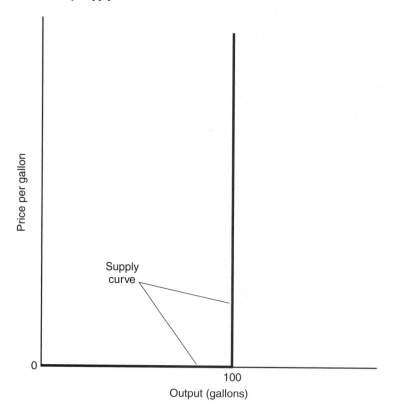

b. The cartel would expand output only so long as marginal revenue exceeds marginal cost. Since marginal cost is zero, this means that the cartel would expand output only so long as marginal revenue is positive. Marginal revenue is as follows.

Output	Total revenue (dollars)	Marginal revenue (dollars)
0	0	
		10
10	100	
		8
20	180	
		6
30	240	
		4
40	280	
		2
50	300	
		0
60	300	
		-2
70	280	
		-4
80	240	
		-6
90	180	
		-8
100	100	

Clearly, the cartel would restrict output to 50 gallons and charge $6 per gallon. (Alternatively, it could set output at 60 gallons, and charge $5 per gallon. The profit would be the same.)

c. If the alternative to the cartel is the arrangement described in part a, each firm would be willing to pay up to $20 per hour to achieve and enforce the cartel. With the cartel, each firm makes $30 per hour, since each produces 5 gallons per hour and charges $6 per gallon. Under the arrangement in part a, each firm makes $10 per hour, since each produces 10 gallons per hour and charges $1 per gallon. Thus, each firm's profit per hour is $20 higher under the cartel.

d. If the cartel sets a price of $6 per gallon, this firm can increase its profits by selling an additional 5 gallons per hour at a price per gallon of $5. But if a substantial number of firms begin to act in this way, the cartel will break apart.

3. The two producers will choose the monopoly output, where marginal revenue equals marginal cost. Since marginal cost equals $2, this means that

$$MR = 10 - 2Q = 2$$

so

$$Q = 8/2 = 4$$

Thus, their combined output will be 4 units per hour.

4. They should set the marginal cost at one firm equal to the marginal cost at each other firm. If firm A produces 4 units, firm B produces 3 units, and firm C produces 4 units, the marginal cost at each firm equals $30. Thus, this seems to be the optimal distribution of output.

5. It meant that the holders of these inventories were unlikely to sell them (and depress the price). Yes, by holding output off the market, producers could maintain prices. No.

6. The price leaders tend to be the largest firms. Also, historical factors play a role, and there is sometimes a tendency for low-cost (or medium-cost) firms to be leaders.

7. Yes. Because of possible entry, for one thing.

CASE FOUR

CATCO Electronics Corporation (USA)
Patrick L. Schul, William A. Cunningham, and Lynn E. Gill

Irvin Bosworth, West Coast Distribution Manager of CATCO Electronics Corporation, stared balefully at the two letters lying before him on the table (Exhibits 1 and 2). Concerned, he poked impatiently at the intercom button.

"Linda, would you get Mr. Kano on the line for me?" Mr. Bosworth was wanting to confer with Yoshi Kano, Assistant to the President of CATCO, Inc., special staff liaison, charged with overseeing the affairs of CATCO Electronics (USA), a division of CATCO, Inc., a large multinational medical electronics firm headquartered in Osaka, Japan.

"Yoshi-san," he began, "I need to talk to you about Speedy Cargo; they're asking for a meeting to discuss a rate increase, and..."

"Wait a minute, Irv." Kano interrupted, "I thought we settled on agreed rates with Speedy Cargo when we met with them last year!"

"We did, Yoshi-san, but apparently times have changed, and now they're asking for not only a rate increase, but some other concessions on detention charges and the like. I've got two letters from their distribution manager, John Patrick, here on my desk explaining the situation and I've scheduled a meeting here with John and his people for next Tuesday."

Yoshi Kano clenched his teeth. "Irv, this creates a real problem for me, especially since I gave CATCO (JAPAN) cost projections on the new budget based on the old rates. How can I go back now with different numbers? It's impossible!"

"I know, Yoshi-san," Irv replied, "it's a tough situation. But they have given us good service. I think we owe them some consideration."

"O.K., Irv, I'll take a second look at the Speedy Cargo situation. But, I'd also like to consider some alternative options. Why don't you spend the rest of the day on this. Find out what our alternatives are, then meet me in the morning at 8:00 A.M. sharp in my office to go over the matter."

On hanging up the phone, Irv remembered that his immediate boss, Wayne Smith, the West Coast Marketing Manager, had been instrumental in CATCO's decision to use Speedy Cargo. In fact, if memory served him right, Wayne was a personal friend of John Patrick of Speedy Cargo. If anyone could help solve this Speedy Cargo problem, Wayne could. Turning back to the telephone, Irv dialed Wayne Smith's number.

EXHIBIT 1   **Letter to Irvin Bosworth**

September 7, 1987

Dear Irv:

For the past 18 months, Speedy Cargo trucking has been providing container trucking services to CATCO Electronics Corporation (USA). We are located close to CATCO, and can conveniently supply CATCO with containers to unload when CATCO opens at 8:00 a.m. We securely lock CATCO's loaded containers overnight inside a burglar alarmed building to protect them from theft. Similarly, we remove all empty containers from CATCO to Speedy Cargo's yard in the evening. Speedy Cargo carries $500,000 cargo insurance on CATCO's containers. Our owner/operator drivers have been willing to work at night and on weekends on several occasions when strikes in the harbor or work delays have necessitated it. CATCO is a very important customer to Speedy Cargo, and we value our association.

Speedy Cargo's rates were guaranteed until October 1, 1987. Now Speedy Cargo must ask CATCO to adjust these rates to meet the needs of Speedy Cargo and our owner/operator drivers. During the past 12 months Speedy Cargo moved 1155 containers for CATCO. During most of this time, Speedy Cargo paid the owner/operator drivers $54 per roundtrip. On July 19th, Speedy Cargo increased the compensation to owner/operator drivers to $60 per roundtrip, or a $6 increase per container.

During 1986–87, Speedy Cargo earned a 3.5 per cent gross margin on trucking revenues of $489,404. Based on trucking industry standards, a minimum of 5% gross margin (95% operating ratio) would be expected by Speedy Cargo as a reasonable return. Adjusting for cost increases we have incurred, and to allow a reasonable rate of return, a rate of $115 per container is requested by Speedy Cargo for 1987–1988.

There is a second area that should be adjusted. Our drivers are paid the same to bring a container to the yard, and then hook up and move the container to CATCO's facility the next morning, as they are to bring the container directly to CATCO from the harbor. This is true also of empty containers taken to Speedy Cargo's yard at night. This results in an inequity for drivers who store containers in the building overnight or pull out empties from CATCO to the yard. I propose that CATCO be billed $15 for respotting containers from the yard to CATCO and from CATCO to the yard. This will compensate the drivers for the extra hook-up and for the extra driving time involved. The number of containers moved averages three in the morning and three empties at night.

For CATCO's convenience, Speedy Cargo advances certain charges and then bills CATCO for reimbursement. Examples are for container demurrage at the pier, trip permits for unlicensed chassis, and forklift charges for loose freight. Because CATCO's payment cycle is about 45 days, CATCO's has use of Speedy Cargo's working capital during that period. I propose that Speedy Cargo bill charges advanced with a 10% surcharge to compensate us for handling the payment and for use of our money. Alternatively, CATCO's could provide Speedy Cargo with a deposit against which charges could be drawn, which could be replenished as needed.

The proposed changes in rates will allow Speedy Cargo to remain competitive in attracting the good owner/operator drivers needed to provide CATCO with excellent service. We have enjoyed working with everyone at CATCO, and look forward to a long and mutually beneficial business relationship.

Sincerely,

John C. Patrick
President

CATCO ELECTRONICS BACKGROUND

Irv Bosworth, Wayne Smith, and Yoshi Kano are all employed by CATCO Electronics Corporation, a large multinational firm based in Osaka, Japan. As indicated, Irv Bosworth is the West Coast Distribution Manager for CATCO Electronics (USA). Wayne Smith, West Coast Marketing Manager, is his immediate boss. Yoshi Kano, Assistant to the President (USA), is a special staff liaison, charged with overseeing the affairs of the United States division of the firm. (Organization charts for both CATCO (USA) and Speedy Cargo are presented in Figure 1.)

In addition to its well-known line of medical computers, the firm is a full-line producer of a diverse mix of electronics products utilized primarily in medical technological applications. Its sales worldwide are over two billion dollars, and sales in the United States are rapidly approaching the half billion mark. Like many other electronics firms, CATCO Electronics had disappointing sales in 1986–1987. However, a turn-around in the economy was expected to produce a better year for 1987–1988. Expectations were that a sales increase of between 10 and 20 percent might be realistic.

EXHIBIT 2   **Second Letter to Irvin Bosworth**

September 9, 1987

Dear Irv:

We have discussed that Speedy Cargo has been experiencing excessive waiting time at some piers to pick up or return CATCO's containers. As the economy has recovered, the volume of containers moving through the harbor has increased significantly. According to forecasts of West Coast traffic in the August issue of Handling and Shipping, these increases are expected to continue. Planned harbor expansion of container cranes and transfer facilities are several years away. The steamship companies so far have resisted keeping the piers open for more than 8 hours per day (the rail ramps are open 24 hours per day).

The result of the increased volume of containers moving through the harbors is that waiting time to pick up a full container or return an empty container has increased at certain piers and for certain steamship companies. I have attached a list of piers, pier operators, and steamships served by each pier, indicating those where we are experiencing excessive waiting (see Attachment).

Planned time to pick up a container from the harbor, deliver it to CATCO, and return the empty to the harbor is $2\frac{1}{2}$ hours. With this turnaround time, a Speedy Cargo owner/operator driver can make from 3 to 4 roundtrips daily for which he is compensated $60 per roundtrip, averaging $1000 per week. This barely compensates the driver for his time, fuel, maintenance, and investment in his tractor.

Recently, at certain piers it has been taking as much as 4 or 5 hours to pick up or return one container. This significantly reduces owner/operators' ability to earn a living, making them reluctant to continue pulling containers. This also requires Speedy Cargo to retain a greater number of drivers to move the same number of CATCO's containers.

Many trucking firms in the harbor area are instituting a charge for waiting in the harbor beyond 2 hours per roundtrip. Firms such as Cargo Trucking and Well Established Freightlines have instituted this charge. Speedy Cargo proposes to institute a $25 per hour charge for time spent waiting over 2 hours for CATCO's containers. This will go to Speedy Cargo owner/operators, not to Speedy Cargo. The charge is set intentionally below what the driver could earn by completing the roundtrip with no waiting. Speedy Cargo will keep stringent control of logged times and stamped gate times to monitor waiting time charged.

Steamship companies either operate their own container transfer stations at the piers, or contract for these services from pier operators. The better steamships provide sufficient cranes and operators (longshoremen) to provide adequate service. They also own an adequate supply of maintained and licensed chassis. Other steamship companies, unfortunately, operate out of congested terminals. If a ship is being worked, cranes are not available to put containers on chassis for delivery to customers. Chassis often are not available, are in poor condition, or are not licensed. When chassis are not licensed properly, we must purchase a trip permit at a cost of $5.

Speedy Cargo often is faced with a choice of accepting a bad order chassis or waiting for a good chassis. If the drivers try to take exceptions for damages on the interchange documents, they must wait to exchange the chassis for a good chassis or pull into a repair facility for repairs. This causes excessive delays. Often, in order to service CATCO's delivery requirements, we have taken bad order chassis. When we return these chassis, exceptions for damages are inevitably taken on the interchange and Speedy Cargo is billed for repairs. We must then either try to resolve the repair charges with the steamship company, or pay the charges in order to avoid being cut off from picking up the steamship's containers. In some cases, we have asked you and our other shippers to intercede with the steamship on our behalf, because shippers have economic power over the steamships whereas we do not.

Shippers such as CATCO have a certain degree of control over waiting time in the harbor by selecting steamships that provide adequate facilities and chassis. I know that certain steamship companies providing lower prices are often accompanied by inferior service in the harbor, an inadequate supply of chassis, and poorly maintained or unlicensed chassis. It is my understanding from some of the other carriers that a few large shippers bill the steamship companies back for waiting time charged by truckers resulting from delays in the harbor. You may wish to consider negotiating this with the steamship companies that you use.

By CATCO (USA) allowing Speedy Cargo Trucking to charge for waiting time, Speedy Cargo will be able to retain and attract a sufficient supply of owner/operator drivers to provide you with the excellent service we have provided before the waiting time problem arose. We look forward to your favorable response.

Sincerely,

John C. Patrick
President

P.S. If you or Mr. Kano would like to ride with a driver for a day to witness the harbor operation first-hand, we can arrange it.

ATTACHMENT
Container Terminals

Waiting Time to Pick-Up or Return Containers

Little or No Waiting

PIER	PORT	OPERATOR	STEAMSHIP
93	San Pedro	Private	American President
208	Terminal Island	Matson	Matson, NYK, Showa
228	Long Beach	Private	Sealand
229	Long Beach	Private	Maersk
230	Long Beach	Private	U.S. Line
232	Terminal Island	Solar International	Yang Ming
246	Long Beach	Pacific Container Terminal	TMM (Mexican), Cosco, Columbus, HK Island, Italian, Char Ching, Star Shipping, Westwood, Yugoslav Line

Intermittent Waiting

127	San Pedro	Los Angeles Container Terminal	K Line, Japan Line, Mitsui OSK, YS Line
243	Long Beach	Long Beach Container Terminal	Korea SS, Seapac OOCL, NOL

Frequent Waiting

234	Long Beach	ITS	Zim, K Line, YS Line, Japan Line, Mitsui OSK, Karlander, Hapag Lloyd, KS Line, CGM, Galleon

Speedy Cargo

MEETING AT SPEEDY CARGO HEADQUARTERS

Paul Ronald leaped to his feet as he saw his boss, Mr. John Patrick, rushing down the hall past his office. Hurrying after him, he shouted, "Hey John! Wait up. I really need to talk to you!"

As John slowed to a fast walk, Paul continued, "We have a real problem with our drivers. I've tried to tell you about it several times before. Several drivers have quit, and when I run ads for owner operators, as soon as they find out that the job includes harbor work as well as pigs, they aren't interested. Especially when I tell them what they will be paid. We are so short of drivers, we can't handle all of the business that comes our way; and the drivers are constantly hitting me up for more money on container moves. We just can't continue like this anymore!"

"What the heck are you talking about?" shouted John angrily as he disappeared through the door to the warehouse. "We just gave those drivers an increase from $54 a round to $60 a round, and we didn't even get a rate increase from CATCO! How the heck can they expect to be paid more when I'm losing money on that account as it is? Paul, as dispatcher, you've just got to take a stronger stance with those drivers."

SPEEDY CARGO BACKGROUND

Speedy Cargo Trucking is a local shorthaul carrier certified by the Public Utility Commission of California as a California contract carrier. However, the majority of its revenue is derived from providing specialized exempt local cartage of trailer on flatcar (TOFC) freight, better known as piggyback trailers or "pigs," and cartage of ocean containers out of the local harbors.

Trailers arrive at the railroad piggyback ramps, where they are unloaded from railroad flatcars. Speedy Cargo hauls the trailers to customers' warehouses for unloading, and then returns the empty trailers back to the railroad. The complete cycle is called a "round." Similarly, Speedy Cargo picks up empty trailers from the railroad ramp, takes them to customers to be loaded, and then delivers the loaded trailers back to the railroad where they are loaded onto flatcars for shipment to eastern points.

Speedy Cargo's harbor business consists of picking up ocean containers on chassis from the steamship companies and delivering those containers to customers for unloading at their warehouses. The empty containers are then returned to the steamship companies' wharfs in Los Angeles and Long Beach harbors. Also, in some cases, empty containers are picked up at the wharfs to be loaded for export shipping.

A third aspect of Speedy Cargo's business is a bobtail trucking operation. Speedy Cargo is a division of Lincoln Warehousing, Inc., a public warehousing firm operating over 300,000 square feet of warehousing and distribution space in Southern California. The bobtail operation exists primarily to deliver freight in the Southern California area. In addition, the bobtail trucks pick up and deliver "loose freight" (freight that is not in ocean containers or that has been unloaded from ocean containers at transit sheds located in the harbor).

Picking up loose freight in the harbor and delivering it requires that drivers load the freight onto their trucks at the transit sheds or container freight stations and also unload the freight at the customer's warehouse. The firms operating the harbor freight transit facilities charge the trucking firm picking up freight for rental of forklifts to bring the freight to the tail of the truck for loading. Forklifts are charged at $20 per hour, and on average two hours are required for loading at the transit shed. Forklift and other charges such as demurrage on freight held in the harbor beyond the "free time" are traditionally advanced by the trucking company and then billed back to customers. Depending upon the payment performance of the customer, these charges may be outstanding from 30 to 60 days. Demurrage charges are also billed by steamship companies for containers held beyond allowed free time in the harbor, usually because the containers are awaiting payment of customs duties and subsequent release by U.S. customs. These charges are also extended by the trucking company and billed back to the customer.

In certain cases, the steamship company also charges the truckline detention for containers and chassis which are held beyond free time (usually three days) for pickup in the harbor, unloading, and return of the empty to the harbor. Sometimes, the shipper holds a container too long, past the one day allowed to unload a container, and is billed for detention by the trucker. In other cases, the trucking company does not return the container from its yard to the harbor on a timely basis and must bear the cost of detention which is typically $8.50 for each day the container is held beyond free time.

In some cases, when there is a congested condition in the harbor and at certain wharfs, the trucker will not return empties in order to get more loaded containers out of the harbor for customers. Returning an empty container may entail delays of two or more hours when volume at wharfs is too great for the cranes and available personnel to handle. The truck driver then bobtails (runs without a container attached) back to the harbor to pick up another full container, and earns revenue only on the loaded leg of the journey. Consequently, later on, an empty container must be taken from the yard to the harbor with no full container available from the return leg out of the harbor. This results in the driver running uncompensated miles. The trucker has a difficult time charging the shipper for detention on empties held in this manner, even though the detention resulted in order to provide expedited delivery service to the shipper when there is congestion at the wharf.

2nd MEETING AT SPEEDY CARGO

Later that day, John Patrick stopped at the dispatcher's office to see Paul Ronald. "I'm sorry I was so short with you, Paul," he began. "This situation with the owner operators really has me upset. I really don't know what they expect me to do. My back is against the wall with CATCO Electronics. CATCO is one of our major accounts and we would really be hurt if we lose them. The trouble is, they know it!"

"I hear what you are saying," Paul responded, "but what am I supposed to tell the owner operators? Is there any chance you could explain to the folks at CATCO that we need to pay the drivers more to keep them?"

"I hope so. But, you know how hard it is to get changes through...what with the confusing way the Japanese make decisions. Let's put our heads together next week and see what arguments we can come up with. In the meantime, here is the year-end profit and loss for the total firm and the trucking division (Exhibit 3), the current container rates for CATCO and the volume of business we had with them last year (Exhibit 4). Look them over, and we'll get together next week to plan our attack."

LATER THAT DAY

Later that day, John Patrick poked his head into the driver ready room and greeted Ray Nicholson, an owner operator driver who has been with Speedy Cargo Trucking for many years. Ray looked a bit solemn.

"How are you doing, Ray?"

"Not so good," Ray answered. "I've been tied up all day at Pier 234 trying to get containers out of the harbor for CATCO. The wait lines are impossible; I got two whole containers delivered. Paul really must be down on my case to stick me with that detail—I'm going broke!"

Squirming in his seat, he continued. "When I get to work pigs, I can do at least five rounds a day without busting my hump, and I average $60 per round. No way can I get by on two loads a day out of the harbor! Some days I get tied up all day for one lousy load, and on good days I can only do 3 or 4 containers a day! I need to gross at least $1,200 per week to make the payment on my tractor, pay my bills, and have something left over for my wife and kids. I'd rather just work on pigs and leave the containers for someone else!"

John looked thoughtful. "It's too bad you are having problems, Ray. Could you help me out with some cost information on handling containers? Maybe I can use it when I talk to Irv Bosworth at CATCO about our rates for next year."

A few days later, John found a cost report, prepared by Ray's accountant, on his desk (Exhibit 5). He wondered how he might be able to make use of it, or if he should invite a driver representative to go with him to the negotiations at CATCO. He made a mental note to discuss this with Paul Ronald when they met next week.

EXHIBIT 3   **Lincoln Warehousing, Inc.**

Statement of Earnings for Year Ended August 30, 1987

	YEAR-TO-DATE	%
Revenue		
Trucking Division	$ 489,404.20	
Warehousing	6,537,821.40	
Expenses (Warehouse division only)		
Salaries	3,399,667.10	52.0
Transportation	588,403.93	9.0
Advertising	65,378.21	1.0
Over, Short, and Damage	98,067.32	1.5
Depreciation	653,782.14	10.0
Interest	915,295.00	14.0
Insurance	163,445.54	2.5
Office Expense	98,067.32	1.5
Taxes and Licenses	26,151.29	0.4
Entertainment and Travel	39,226.93	0.6
Total	$6,047,484.80	92.5
Income	490,336.61	7.5
Revenue		
Charges Advanced for Customers	$ 19,469.75	
Trucking Revenue	469,934.45	
Total	$489,404.20	100.00
Expenses		
Salaries	38,920.10	8.0
Advertising	2,065.10	0.4
Automobile Expense	1,432.89	0.3
Charges Advanced for Customers	19,882.26	4.0
Owner Operators	335,016.99	72.5
Damages, Demurrage, Shortage	3,589.80	0.7
Equipment Rentals	1,178.00	0.2
Insurance	10,363.08	2.1
Office Expense	1,930.00	0.4
Postage	617.34	0.1
Rent	29,736.00	6.1
Taxes and Licenses	500.00	0.1
Telephone	5,613.35	1.1
Travel and Entertainment	1,648.11	0.3
Total	$472,493.37	96.5
Income	$ 16,910.83	3.5

ONE WEEK LATER

John Patrick hunched over the conference table and peered at Paul Ronald over the top of his glasses. "Well, Paul," he questioned, "where do you think we ought to head with our preparations to work this deal out with CATCO? I understand they've asked for a meeting next Tuesday to discuss the situation."

Paul rubbed his chin thoughtfully and began tentatively, "First, John, there are a few things I need to understand before we get into this thing. First off, I was surprised at how much we pay for insurance!"

"It does seem like a bunch," John agreed. "Of course that covers all of our liability insurance, as well as cargo insurance. For most shippers, we carry cargo insurance of $50,000 per container. Because the value of the cargo in most containers is less than that, we pay a minimum of $5,000 per year for cargo insurance, and then it's adjusted at the end of the year to one percent of freight billings."

"CATCO is a different matter. Because of their high value cargo, we need to carry cargo insurance in the amount of $500,000 per container. We report that separately, and that insurance policy runs 6 percent of revenue billing on CATCO's business."

"Wow! They do sock it to us on high value cargo. But I guess that the insurance cost per container is reasonable in relation to the possible loss of a container. Is it reflected in the rates? By the way, how did you ever come up with rates based on so many containers per month?"

"Well, Paul, that happened a few months before you arrived on the scene. Irv Bosworth called me in for a meeting with Yoshi Kano, their Assistant to the President in Japan. They informed me that they had a bid from a competing firm to provide service on the basis of the number of containers moved, and what did I want to do about it? We were getting $92 a round before that."

EXHIBIT 4

1986–87 Container Rates for CATCO Electronics (USA)	
First 60 containers per month	$92
Next 61–90 containers (monthly)	85
Over 91 containers (monthly)	55

1986–87 Containers Moved for CATCO Electronics (USA)	
October 1986	89
November	50
December	62
January 1987	71
February	86
March	120
April	84
May	99
June	144
July	142
August	119
September	89
Total	1155

EXHIBIT 5   **Analysis of Owner-Operator Costs**

CAPACITY		
	3 round trips/day	
	5 days/week	
	15 trips/week	
	52 weeks/year	
	780 trips/year	
ALLOCATED COSTS		PER ROUND TRIP
Maintenance	$3,600/year	$4.61
Major Repairs	2,400/year	3.08
Insurance	3,000/year	3.85
Taxes	720/year	.92
License	2,650/year	3.40
FUEL	20 mile round trip	
	÷5 MPG	
	4 gallons @ $1.10	4.40
LABOR		
$10/hr × 1.42 fringe		
& taxes =	$14.20	
	10 hrs/day	
	$140.20	
divided by 3 trips/day	3	46.73
Amortization		
$20,000.00 tractor		
÷4 years		
$ 5,000.00 amortization		
780 trips		6.41
COST FOR OWNER-OPERATOR PER ROUND TRIP		$73.40

"I had a meeting with the drivers to figure out what we should do—meet the price or bow out. They voted to take a cut from $60 to $54 a round to keep the business. Of course, about the only one of our 10 drivers still around that remembers that is Ray Nicholson!"

"Another thing," Paul continued. "What's this charge for rent on the statement? The trucking operations shares facilities with warehousing—how can we get socked with a charge for rent? If we weren't in trucking, the space we use would still be there! It's not fair to charge that to us, and it makes us look not very profitable."

"I hear what you are saying," John answered in a surprised tone. "We charge the trucking operation for an acre of yard space for storing empties, for the space required to store loaded containers inside the building, and of course for office space you occupy."

"When we leased the building, we looked for one with enough yard space for our trucking operation. And, I might add, the trucking P & L statement does not include a charge for general expenses and administration. That's carried as burden in its own cost center. At our current sales volume, G & A runs about 10 percent of total sales."

The meeting continued for several hours of give and take to iron out an approach to renegotiation of next year's rates with CATCO.

2nd MEETING AT CATCO HEADQUARTERS

Irv Bosworth and Wayne Smith were both in Yoshi Kano's office 8:00 sharp the morning following their initial meeting. Irv spun the two letters from Speedy Cargo Trucking (Exhibits 1 and 2) onto Kano's desk. "Look these over when you get a chance, Yoshi-san. In the meantime, to refresh your memory, here are Speedy Cargo's current rates and the number of containers we moved last year (Exhibit 4)."

After skimming over John Patrick's two letters, Yoshi Kano responded, "Gentlemen, if I remember correctly, when Speedy Cargo took over our trucking business from Port Container Pullers last year, they agreed to meet the rate that had been proposed by Japan Overseas Trucklines, a rate of $92 per container for the first 60 containers, $85 for the next 30, and $55 for over 90 containers per month. Is this not the case?"

"This is true, Yoshi-san," Wayne responded. "But let's set the record straight. While Port did work out good for us for a few years, they went belly up on an $85 rate. While we started Speedy Cargo at a higher rate of $92 per container, we required them to carry $500,000 cargo insurance, a substantially higher level than the standard $50,000 coverage. As you know, this request was based on our experience of having a container stolen out of Port Container's yard. John Patrick told me the insurance coverage costs Speedy Cargo an extra $7 per container, which they tacked onto what we were paying Port. Of course, after we hit them with the proposal from Japan Overseas, that cost just got folded into the rate. Apparently they're just not able to provide the necessary service under these rates and

conditions. All I hear about is the troubles they're having getting all of our containers out of the harbor, how congested some of the wharfs are and the trouble Speedy Cargo has attracting and keeping good drivers. That's really their major problem."

Pointing his finger out at Wayne, Kano angrily replied, "Wayne, you and I both know that Japan makes all the decisions about what steamship lines to use. We simply abide by their decisions at this end. I'm sick of hearing that excuse!"

"Look Wayne," Kano continued, "I don't mean to fly off the handle like this. But you know the pressure we have been getting from both ends over this new Just-in-Time inventory technique. The whole industry, including our customers, is insisting we provide more frequent deliveries in smaller quantities. Our biggest customer, Logon Manufacturing, Inc., is shoving this whole JIT thing down our throat, and Japan agrees with them. They keep referring to us as 'partners in production,' but they want this extra service with almost no price increase. Japan feels that the entire industry will force JIT on all suppliers and we might as well gear up for the change."

Irv looked confused. "I know our sales force has been throwing around this Just-in-Time thing, but I'm not sure what it is or how it will affect us."

"I've been aware of this problem," stated Kano. "We Japanese live by the JIT philosophy but Americans are just now beginning to see the light. That's why I asked Bill Kanban, our West Coast Head of Operations, to prepare a report on JIT and how it will impact on our company. You should have that report (Exhibit 6) by this afternoon. In the meantime, let's get back to our problem at hand."

Irv responded, "I really wonder if their 10 drivers are enough to take care of us, especially when the end of the month rolls around and we get our usual end-of-the-month peak inflow of containers. Good Lord, we might have 40 containers in one

EXHIBIT 6   **Memo from Bill Kanban**

TO: All West Coast Managers
FROM: Bill Kanban, Head of Operations
SUBJECT: Just-in-Time
DATE: September 9, 1987

In response to a request from Yoshi Kano, this memo is an attempt to briefly describe the Just-in-Time inventory philosophy now being implemented by most of our major customers. Also included is the impact this will mean to our operations. JIT has been utilized extensively by Japanese firms, including our parent company.

The basic philosophy behind JIT is that inventory is waste. Under JIT, orders are placed on relatively fixed schedules from suppliers, but in smaller and more frequent orders. The orders should arrive JUST IN TIME to be used in production. Inventory holding costs are to be eliminated or minimized.

In order for JIT not to simply be an excuse to push inventory back on us, our customers will work closely with us on their production needs. Since the majority of our sales are to firms located in Silicon Valley, our effective delivery radius is only 150 miles or 4 hours one way. As a result we feel we can safely guarantee 2 deliveries per day within a $1\frac{1}{2}$ to 2 hour time window, as opposed to our traditional 2 deliveries per week. With our proposed changes in transportation equipment, including using a mixture of our own and for-hire trucks, costs of providing this service should not increase above the 5 to 7 per cent range. Our first customer that will go to this schedule is D.K. Systems, who have indicated that they would be willing to renegotiate prices up to a 10% increase if we can live up to these performance standards. If our research is correct on our additional costs, this is a potential 3 to 5 percent increase in profitability. This is, however, a big if. As you know, over 90% of our sales come from 3 products—medfax communicators, digital blood delivery monitors, and medtech desktop computers. But, our shipments from Japan are full containers of only one item. Thus, to fill a complete order, no matter how big or small, will normally require 3 separate containers. It is not that uncommon to have to hold up several orders and trucks waiting for a container to be delivered from the port. Whatever the reason for the delay, this costs us money. Our drivers are teamsters and they cost us $21.76 per hour including fringes regardless of whether they are driving or not because the order is not ready. Given what the detention combined with waiting time costs are for the regulated carriers we use, their time sitting around drinking coffee is $13.79 per hour.

With our new proposed JIT delivery schedule this simply cannot happen. Therefore, the only insurance we can use is inventory, which runs counter to the JIT philosophy. More important, it is much more costly, and cost increases were not figured in when we arrived at the above estimates. Each container is worth about $500,000 to $750,000 and our inventory carrying costs run about 25 percent, as can be seen from the accompanying attachment. Japan only ships full containers,

CASE FOUR

and we cannot store less than full containers for any length of time—due to our warehouse limitation. Any safety stock that we would contemplate keeping would be in container minimums.

I am aware of the problem expressed by Speedy Cargo concerning delay times at the docks. The same problem exists at the Japanese ports. I have spoken with Chet Haire who handles all outgoing shipments from the parent company. He is negotiating with On Time freight forwarders to handle the scheduling of all shipments, and promises that this problem will be taken care of in the next couple of months. However, it would be wise if we checked this out with whatever carrier we decide to use.

To sum up, I am confident that we can handle the transition to a JIT system within the costs outlined above. The "weakest link," as I see it, is the level and consistency of container deliveries from the ships. If this is resolved, then implementing a JIT system can be done efficiently.

ship and the merchandise is already sold when it arrives! We need to get all that merchandise to the distribution center and shipped to make our month's end sales quota, and you know what CATCO (JAPAN) says when we don't. Paul Ronald, the Speedy Cargo dispatcher, always gives me a bunch of bull about CATCO being 'Number One,' but when we have a full warehouse crew ready to unload freight and the containers don't arrive as planned, I really wonder! I just want all our merchandise delivered on time, with no headaches!"

"I know we used Well Established Freightliners for many years prior to switching over to Port. Are they still around, Irv?" Kano queried.

"As a matter of fact, I talked to Glenn Canary over at Well Established yesterday. He indicated they would be more than willing to take on the business, but their rates are way out of line at $125 per container. I know they give great service; they own their own trucks you know; but they just can't compete with nonunion carriers."

"Anyone else?" pressed Kano.

"Well, I talked to Lenny Solox over at Solox Trucklines. I was favorably impressed with this guy. He wanted the business and would provide it for $92 per container. As far as getting the job done, he said he could

get all the drivers we wanted...no problem."

"Solox also uses owner operators and not their own trucks. Lenny used to work for Well Established before he started his own firm. They have been in business for about 2 years now. Since both Solox and Speedy Cargo use the same source of drivers, I wonder how Lenny can guarantee drivers where John Patrick is having so much trouble. You know how the trucking business has been around here since deregulation. We've got more firms to pick from and rate discounts are rampant. However, a lot of these new trucklines are only around for a couple of years or less before they go belly-up. Their cash flow is so bad they resort to buying freight, even at a loss, just to have the cash coming in."

Wayne interrupted, "After Irv and I talked the other day about this problem, I called up Beth Logan over at Medco Systems, one of our competitors. She is their traffic manager and we have known each other for quite a while. They have used Speedy Cargo, Well Established and Solox for their deliveries, and Beth has kept a record of their performance on some vendor quality program she has for her personal computer. After a little sweet talking—"

"And a $135.00 dinner charged on your company VISA," laughed Irv.

EXHIBIT 7 **Vendor Quality Report Summary**

	SPEEDY CARGO	SOLOX	WELL ESTABLISHED
Average Transit Time	7	5	7
Truck Availability	5	5	9
Price	8	9	4
Reliability	7	4	7
Loss & Damage	7	5	8
Special Services	6	6	8
Claims Settlement	5	3	7
Bill Accuracy	6	4	8

"Yes," agreed Wayne, "Things I do for CATCO. Anyway, she agreed to give me a very abbreviated summary of their quality assessment of three carriers."

As Wayne passed out the report (Exhibit 7), he continued, "Although the report is somewhat general, I think it gives us an idea of how the three truckers rank relative to each other, at least as far as Beth sees it. It won't answer our problems for us, but it's the best I could get for $135.00. At least it gives us a basis on which to compare services."

Looking over the figures, Kano responded, "Wayne, I believe we are in a tough situation here. While I recognize the need for developing stronger continuity with our vendors, I am still very reticent to change the budget figures unless it's absolutely necessary. You must recognize my situation. However, given our discussion here, I do believe that we need to at least meet with Speedy Cargo to discuss their concerns. Before we meet, however, I want you and Irv to put your heads together and take a closer look at the inherent validity and impact on our operations of the Speedy Cargo proposals before we get to the table."

Questions

1. Is CATCO Electronics a perfectly competitive firm? A monopolist? Is Speedy Cargo a perfectly competitive firm? A monopolist?

2. Does Speedy Cargo engage in price discrimination?

3. If Speedy Cargo moves over 91 containers in a particular month for CATCO Electronics, does its revenue per container for those containers exceeding 91 cover its costs?

4. What are the costs and benefits to Yoshi Kano of changing the budget figures? Are they different from the costs and benefits to CATCO Electronics of such a change?

5. With the existing rates, is Speedy Cargo likely to continue operations?

6. If you were Yoshi Kano, would you approve the rate increase for Speedy Cargo? Why or why not?

7. If you were John Patrick, would you continue to deliver cargo for CATCO Electronics if CATCO refuses to approve the rate increase? Why or why not?

CHAPTER 11

Game Theory

Chapter Profile

Game theory attempts to study decision making in situations where there is a mixture of conflict and cooperation, as in oligopoly. A game is a competitive situation where two or more persons pursue their own interests, and no person can dictate the outcome. For example, poker is a game, and so is a situation in which two firms are engaged in competitive R and D programs.

A game is described in terms of the players, the rules of the game, the payoffs of the game, and the information conditions that exist during the game. The relevant features of a two-person game can be shown by constructing a **payoff matrix**. If each firm has a **dominant strategy**, this strategy is its best choice regardless of what other firms do. Not all games have a dominant strategy for each firm. An **equilibrium** exists when no player has an incentive to unilaterally change his or her strategy.

In a **Nash equilibrium**, each firm adopts a strategy that is its best choice given what the other firms do. Some games do not have a Nash equilibrium; others have more than one Nash equilibrium.

The **prisoner's dilemma** is a type of game useful in analyzing oligopolistic situations, such as whether cartel members should cheat. If the game is played once, there are strong incentives to cheat, but if it is repeated, other strategies may be better. The **folk theorem** states that any type of behavior can be supported by an equilibrium as long as there is a high probability of future interaction. **Incomplete information games** loosen the restrictive assumption that all players have the same information. There are also **coordination games,** where managers coordinate with others, either within a firm or among firms in a market. A scenario of strict competition where any gain by one player is matched by losses for the other is known as a **zero-sum game** and may be a characteristic of a mature industry where there is little room for market growth.

Managers want to pursue strategic foresight; this is the ability to make decisions today that are rational, conditioned on the anticipated future behavior of other. Game theory models this foresight through backward induction, where a manager would go to the end result of the game to determine what strategy players will use and then choose actions for the current period that are rational, given the belief about the future.

Managers must pay attention only to credible signals from rivals. Game theory can be used to help determine the credibility of threats, promises, and commitments.

Questions

Completion

1. If each player has a(n) _____ strategy, this strategy is its best choice regardless of what other players do.

2. In a(n) _____ equilibrium, each player adopts a strategy that is its best choice given what the other players do.

3. In the prisoner's dilemma, the dominant strategy for each prisoner is to _____.

4. If the game of the prisoner's dilemma is repeated indefinitely, the best strategy for each player may not be to _____.

5. There will always be an alternative equilibrium where both players are _____ off in the prisoner's dilemma.

6. A commitment tends to be more persuasive if it seems _____ and _____.

7. Not _____ games have a dominant strategy for every player.

8. If one player can convince the other player that he or she is _____ going to take the course of action that maximizes his or her profit, that player can sometimes make a threat credible.

9. A firm may succeed in convincing a potential entrant not to enter its market by _____ its own profits if it does not resist entry.

10. Firms often try to commit themselves _____ to a particular move, even if they cannot be _____ to actually carry out this move.

True or False

_____ 1. To be credible, a firm's commitments must be backed up with the assets and expertise required to carry out the commitment.

_____ 2. Firms frequently send signals to one another indicating their intentions, motives, and objectives.

_____ 3. Firms can never alter the payoff matrix.

_____ 4. A firm may succeed in convincing a potential entrant not to enter its market by reducing its own profits if it does not resist entry.

_____ 5. A firm may set a low price to signal potential entrants that it is a very low-cost producer.

_____ 6. In many situations, the firm that makes the first move has a substantial advantage.

_____ 7. A Nash equilibrium exists for any and every game.

_____ 8. A Nash equilibrium will result in a two-player game where both players have a dominant strategy.

_____ 9. A Nash equilibrium will result in a two-player game where neither players has a dominant strategy.

Multiple Choice

1. A government, by subsidizing one of its firms, can:

    a. change the payoff matrix in a particular market
    b. induce foreign firms to withdraw from the market
    c. get other governments to retaliate
    d. all of the above
    e. none of the above

2. A dominant strategy is a strategy where:

    a. the player loses
    b. a second-best approach is used
    c. pure strategies are mixed with impure strategies
    d. all of the above
    e. none of the above

3. Games may have:

    a. a Nash equilibrium
    b. no Nash equilibrium
    c. more than one Nash equilibrium
    d. a dominant strategy for each player
    e. all of the above

4. A strategic move may be:

    a. threatening to the firm's rivals
    b. nonthreatening to the firm's rivals
    c. met with substantial retaliation by the firm's rivals
    d. met with little or no retaliation by the firm's rivals
    e. all of the above

5. A firm may be able to deter entry into its market by:

    a. building excess production capacity
    b. gaining a reputation for "irrational" resistance to entry
    c. threatening to resist even though potential entrants believe that it is
       not in this firm's interest to resist
    d. only a and b
    e. all of the above

6. If two rival firms both adopt a preemptive strategy with regard to capacity
   expansion:

    a. each tries to expand before the other does so
    b. there may be two Nash equilibria
    c. both firms are likely to profit greatly if the demand for the product grows
       more slowly than expected
    d. both a and b
    e. all of the above

7. If a firm can convince its rivals that it is unequivocally committed to a particular move:

   a. they may be convinced that they would lose more than they would gain from a protracted struggle
   b. they may back down without retaliating
   c. they may engage in moves designed to counter this firm's move
   d. both a and b
   e. all of the above

Problems

1. Firms E and F are duopolists. They each have two possible strategies for product development. The payoff matrix is as follows:

Possible strategies for firm E	Possible strategies for firm F	
	A	*B*
1	Firm E's profit: $5 million Firm F's profit: $6 million	Firm E's profit: $4 million Firm F's profit: $5 million
2	Firm E's profit: $6 million Firm F's profit: $5 million	Firm E's profit: $5 million Firm F's profit: $4 million

   a. What is firm E's optimal strategy?
   b. What is firm F's optimal strategy?
   c. Is this an example of the prisoner's dilemma?
   d. Is there a dominant strategy for firm E? Explain.
   e. Is there a dominant strategy for firm F? Explain.

2. If two players are engaged in a game with characteristics of the prisoner's dilemma, can the equilibrium depend on whether the game is played repeatedly or just once? Explain.

3. Firms A and B agree to maintain their prices at the monopoly level. In the event that either cheats on this agreement, both firms will adopt a strategy of "tit for tat." Describe how each firm may attempt to determine whether the other firm is cheating.

4. If the payoff matrix is as follows, what strategy will firm I choose? What strategy will firm II choose?

Possible strategies for firm I	Possible strategies for firm II		
	1	*2*	*3*
	[Profits for firm I, or losses for firm II (dollars)]		
A	$10	$9.0	$11
B	8	8.5	10

5. Firms C and D are about to stage rival advertising campaigns, and each firm has a choice of strategies. The payoff matrix follows.

Possible strategies for firm C	Possible strategies for firm D	
	1	*2*
A	Firm C's profit: $7 million Firm D's profit: $10 million	Firm C's profit: $6 million Firm D's profit: $7 million
B	Firm C's profit: $8 million Firm D's profit: $7 million	Firm C's profit: $7 million Firm D's profit: $8 million

   a.   Does firm C have a dominant strategy? If so, what is it?
   b.   Does firm D have a dominant strategy? If so, what is it?
   c.   Is there a Nash equilibrium? If so, what is it?

6.   The Brooks Company's managers begin to sense that the Harris Corporation may attempt to enter their market.

   a.   What steps might they take to dissuade Harris from doing so?
   b.   What factors are likely to determine whether they will succeed?
   c.   What actions that they have taken (or not taken) in the past may play an important role in influencing whether or not Harris tries to enter?

7.   The Miller Company must decide whether to advertise its product or not. If its rival, Morgan Corporation, decides to advertise its product, Miller will make $4 million if it advertises and $2 million if it does not advertise. If Morgan does not advertise, Miller will make $5 million if it advertises and $3 million if it does not.

   a.   Is it possible to determine the payoff matrix? Why or why not?
   b.   Can you tell whether Miller has a dominant strategy? If so, what is it?

8.   The Adams Company has two possible strategies, and the Burr Company has two possible strategies. The payoff matrix follows.

Possible strategies for Adams Company	Possible strategies for Burr Company	
	1	*2*
A	Adams' profit: −$20 million Burr's profit: −$20 million	Adams' profit: $40 million Burr's profit: $20 million
B	Adams' profit: $20 million Burr's profit: $40 million	Adams' profit: −$20 million Burr's profit: −$20 million

   a.   If the Adams Company has the first move, what strategy is it likely to choose? What strategy is Burr likely to choose?
   b.   If the Burr Company has the first move, what strategy is it likely to choose? What strategy is Adams likely to choose?

Answers

Completion

   1. dominant   2. Nash   3. confess   4. confess   5. better   6. binding, irreversible   7. all   8. not   9. reducing   10. first, first

True or False

1. True   2. True   3. False   4. True   5. True   6. True   7. False   8. False
9. False

Multiple Choice

1. d   2. e   3. e   4. e   5. d   6. d   7. e

Problems

1. a. Strategy 2.
    b. Strategy A.
    c. No.
    d. Yes. Strategy 2.
    e. Yes. Strategy A.

2. Yes. See the text.

3. In some cases, trade associations have been authorized to collect detailed information concerning each firm's transactions.

4. Firm I will choose strategy A. Firm II will choose strategy 2.

5. a. Yes. Strategy B.
    b. No.
    c. Yes. Firm C chooses strategy B and firm D chooses strategy 2.

6. a. They might signal Harris that they will fight hard to resist its entry into their market. They might build extra productive capacity and do other things to convince Harris that the payoff matrix is such that, if Harris enters, it will be more profitable for Brooks to resist than not to resist.
    b. It will depend on how convinced Harris is that Brooks really will resist if Harris enters, and on how effective Harris believes such resistance would be.
    c. If Brooks has a reputation for fighting hard in the past to resist entry, this may be important.

7. a. No. We are not given Morgan's profit figures.
    b. Yes. Its dominant strategy is to advertise.

8. a. Strategy A. Strategy 2.
    b. Strategy 1. Strategy B.

CHAPTER 12

Auctions

Chapter Profile

The amount of income generated by auctions in the United States has increased dramatically; it is increasingly important for managers to understand auctions' underlying mechanisms and decision rules. Much of the increase in auction revenue can be attributed to two factors: Auctions can vastly improve a manager's information about purchasers' demand and reservation prices and the advent of increased utilization of the Internet, which allows for a larger bidding pool in a virtual world.

Repurchase tender offers (RTOs) are an example of auctions that both gain information and generate the highest reservation prices. As several studies have shown, the average premium paid for tendered shares is 25–30 percent lower under modified Dutch auctions than under a **fixed-price system**. The growth in Internet-enabled auctions is led by decreased transaction and operational costs. Both aspects of this growth argue for more attention to auction mechanisms in the management suite.

One of the potential failings of auctions is that there is no recontracting allowed. Nonetheless, if operated efficiently, auctions will lead sellers (producers) to higher levels of profitability and producer surplus than fixed-price systems.

Four basic auction mechanisms exist: **ascending-price** or English auction; **descending-price** or Dutch auction; **first-price, sealed-bid**; and **second-price, sealed-bid**. Under basic assumptions regarding risk neutrality and information symmetry, all four mechanisms (when efficient) will lead to the same winning bid (the reservation price of the second-highest bidder).

For English and second-price, sealed-bid auctions, bidders have a dominant strategy—always bid up to the **reservation price**. For Dutch auctions and first-price, sealed-bid auctions, there is no dominant strategy, but under the assumption of rationality, a Nash equilibrium exists and the optimal strategy of a bidder is clear—estimate the reservation price of the second-highest bidder and bid that price.

From the seller (producer) perspective, the key to running an auction successfully is in identifying the information that becomes available under such a system. Typically, the decision rule for sellers is to choose the level of output that equates marginal revenue to marginal cost. However, given that auctions are often run for very few units (typically one), this mechanism is not helpful. Rather, what the manager should focus on is the distribution of reservation prices across bidders and set opening price equal to the value of the item plus one-half of the highest expected reservation price. Beyond this, the simplest step the seller can undertake is to increase the number of bidders, as producer surplus cannot decrease with additional bidders. However, if the seller has reason to believe that the bidders are **risk averse** (to not winning the auction), they should choose a first-price, sealed-bid auction to maximize their profit.

Questions

Completion

1. When a buyer announces the need for a product or service and sellers bid for the right to sell the buyer the good or service, we have a(n) _____ auction.

2. Two special cases of the ascending-bid (English) auction are the _____ auction and the ascending-bid _____ auction.

3. The initial price set by the seller at an auction is called the seller's _____ price.

4. The initial price in a Dutch auction is set very _____.

5. A second-price, sealed-bid auction is also called a(n) _____ auction.

6. Bidders that bid to maximize expected values and not risk-adjusted utility are risk _____.

7. In efficient first-bid ascending auctions, the highest bidder receives the item at the reservation price of the _____.

8. Incentive compatible rules are those that encourage bidders to reveal their _____.

9. A decision rule to estimate the reservation price of the second-highest bidder and bid that is optimal in a(n) _____-price, sealed-bid auction.

10. In an ascending auction, managerial action is similar to _____-degree price discrimination.

11. If bidders are risk averse, then a manager should use a(n) _____-price auction.

12. The phenomenon of a successful bidder who later realizes that the true value of the item purchased is less than the price paid is called the _____.

True or False

_____ 1. Due to the lack of recontracting, auctions may yield *nonpareto* equilibria.

_____ 2. All else being equal, expected revenue can never decrease with the presence of additional bidders.

_____ 3. The initial price in a Dutch auction is set equal to the seller's reservation price.

_____ 4. The price paid by the winning bidder in a second-price, sealed-bid auction equals his or her reservation price.

_____ 5. Bidders in private-value auctions value the auctioned goods similarly.

_____ 6. Bidders in common-value auctions value the auctioned goods similarly.

_____ 7. The dominant strategy in a Dutch auction is to always be willing to bid up to your reservation price.

_____ 8. The dominant strategy in an English auction is to bid your reservation price.

_____ 9. There is no dominant strategy in a first-price, sealed-bid auction.

_____ 10. The optimal strategy in a Dutch auction is to estimate the reservation price of the second highest bidder and bid that.

_____ 11. Both English and second-price, sealed-bid auctions are ruled by the same dominant strategy.

_____ 12. In second-price auctions, risk preferences do not influence bidding strategy.

_____ 13. In first-price auctions, risk preferences do not influence bidding strategy.

Multiple Choice

1. The winner's curse means:

   a. the winner pays more than the object's true value
   b. the winner will go into debt
   c. the auctioneer loses revenue
   d. a lack of information about the object
   e. none of the above

2. Which of the following is not a recognized auction mechanism?

   a. Dutch
   b. English
   c. Vickrey
   d. second-price, sealed-bid
   e. none of the above

3. The difference between common-value and private-value auctions is:

   a. that one is ascending and the other is descending
   b. information symmetry
   c. the level of risk aversion of bidders
   d. knowledge of the true value of the good
   e. none of the above

4. A bidder should bid his or her reservation price in:

   a. a first-price, sealed-bid auction
   b. an English auction
   c. a second-price, sealed-bid auction
   d. a and b
   e. none of the above

5. In which of the following auction types does the bidder have a dominant strategy?

   a. Vickrey
   b. Dutch
   c. first-price, sealed-bid
   d. none of the above

Problems

1. Using calculus, prove that, if a seller's expected revenue in an auction is given by

$$B = \left[\frac{N-1}{N+1} \right] \text{(reservation price of bidder)}$$

   the bid cannot decrease as the number of bidders (N) increases.

2. Assuming that a producer has four units to sell and the marginal cost of production is constant at $0, calculate the consumer and producer surplus arising from the posted price and auction in the following table.

	Auction		Posted Price	
Consumer	Reservation price	Winning bid	Consumer	Price paid
1	$50	$31	1	$50
2	$30	—	2	—
3	$100	$71	3	$50
4	$70	$61	4	$50
5	$60	$51	5	$50
Consumer surplus				
Producer surplus				
Total surplus		$200		$200

3. Calculate the expected profit, given the information in the following table.

Option	Probability of realization	Profit
A	0.25	$100,000
B	0.60	$75,000
C	0.15	$25,000

Answers

Completion
1. reverse   2. Japanese, timed   3. reservation   4. high   5. Vickrey
6. neutral   7. second-highest bidder   8. true preferences   9. first   10. third
11. first   12. winner's curse

True or False
1. True   2. True   3. False   4. False   5. False   6. True   7. False   8. False
9. True   10. True   11. True   12. True   13. False

Multiple Choice

1. a 2. e 3. e 4. c 5. a

Problems

1. $B = \left[\dfrac{N-1}{N+1}\right]$ (reservation price of bidder)

$\dfrac{\partial B}{\partial N} = \left[\dfrac{(N+1) - (N-1)}{(N+1)^2}\right]$ (reservation price of bidder)

$\dfrac{\partial B}{\partial N} > 0$

2.

Consumer	*Auction* Reservation price	Winning bid	*Posted Price* Consumer	Price paid
1	$50	$31	1	$50
2	$30	—	2	—
3	$100	$71	3	$50
4	$70	$61	4	$50
5	$60	$51	5	$50
Consumer surplus		**66**		**80**
Producer surplus		**134**		**120**
Total surplus		$200		$200

3. $73,750

CASE FIVE

How Technology Tailors Price Tags
David Wessel

Charging every consumer the same posted price was a 19th-century innovation that took time to spread. Not so long ago, a tailor on New York's Lower East Side would say in a thick East European accent, "For you, a special price."

You, of course, had no way of telling whether that "special price" was high or low. So you'd haggle and, if the salesman was any good, you'd walk away with a suit and a sense that you had gotten a bargain, even if you hadn't.

Then came stores that charged everyone the same no-haggling-allowed price. Now, technology is attacking that—and not just on the Internet or for air fares.

Faster computers, more sophisticated analysis and huge amounts of data that retailers are collecting allow grocers, drugstores, mortgage lenders, computer makers and other merchants to charge you a "special price" without exactly saying so.

Just because technology makes this possible doesn't mean it will happen soon. Pricing managers across the economy were spooked by the uproar that followed Amazon.com's experiment last fall with charging different prices for the same DVD on the same day. Consumer worries about privacy limit retailers' willingness and, sometimes, ability to use data they've collected.

And there will be losers: Consumers who are charged less won't complain; those charged more may.

But smart merchants are relearning the tailor's savvy about the customer's perceptions. "Amazon.com's biggest mistake was getting caught," says Jared Blank, an analyst at Jupiter Media Matrix Inc. in New York. Don't charge anyone more, consultants advise. Just charge some less. It sounds impossible, yet that's how coupons work, and that's what is happening as computers turn pricing from art to science.

Pricing changed when airline deregulation in 1978 forced airlines to compete on price. At the time, air travel seemed a special case. The product is perishable; an empty seat can't be sold later. Prices were posted electronically and thus were easy to change. In 1985, American Airlines figured out how to adjust prices automatically to maximize revenue. Other airlines, hotel chains and rental-car companies followed. Airlines weren't unique.

Any merchant would love to sell a product at the highest price each customer will pay. A store might price a dress at $300 and sell three even though one customer might be willing to pay $500, and another $400. The trick: Make identical dresses seem different and price each one differently.

David Wessel, "How Technology Tailors Price Tags," from *The Wall Street Journal*, June 21, 2001.

Airlines perfected this. A tourist who books a month in advance pays less than an executive who booked the day before yet both arrive at the same instant.

E-commerce appeared an ideal way to do the same elsewhere, and to some extent it has. Dell Computer Corp. charges one price on its Web site for small firms, another on a site for local government. eBay auctions set prices one buyer at a time. PNC Bank in Pittsburgh auctions certificates of deposit as small as $5,000; if your bid is among the 25 best, you get it.

Online retailing didn't change the world as fast as it was supposed to. But the big action in pricing is off the Internet, and that's where most people shop.

Until recently, big mortgage lenders offered every accepted applicant the same interest rate. Today, their computers draw increasingly fine distinctions and are programmed to offer higher-rate mortgages to slightly riskier applicants who otherwise would have been turned away.

The small initiative generates good public relations because borrowers otherwise would have paid even more elsewhere. But the technology opens the door to charging every applicant a rate based on his or her individual risk. Computers make separating sterling risks from ordinary risks easy. The obstacle: Charging the best risks (read rich) a bit less and others a bit more is ugly. But it's probably inevitable.

Grocery stores appear to be the model of one price for all. But even today, they post one price, charge another to shoppers willing to clip coupons and a third to those with frequent-shopper cards that allow stores to collect detailed data on buying habits. With help from firms armed with Ph.D.s and sophisticated software, big chains use that data to boost revenue by raising some prices and cutting others.

The next steps are already in sight. "Pricing is moving from the product to the store to the individual consumer," says grocery-industry veteran Patrick Kiernan. Some chains automatically dispatch dia-per coupons when a frequent shopper buys baby food but not diapers. Next: Once the computer notes that a regular customer stocks up on Progresso tomato sauce every time it goes on sale, the computer will simply offer the sales price automatically at the cash register whether it's on sale or not.

Before long, the only person paying the posted price—the "insult price," Mr. Kiernan calls it—will be a stranger or a customer who prizes privacy so much she'll pay extra for it.

Questions

Discuss the implications of the trends mentioned in the article from the point of view of:

1. Price discrimination: What type of price discrimination is now more easily done by using computer technology? What are the economic implications of this? What is the likely reaction of consumers? Were consumers getting a "bargain" before companies used this new tool (explain in terms of the consumer surplus)?

2. What government actions, if any, might occur in the future to control these trends? Would regulatory policies to curb this type of price discrimination be justified on the basis of competitive economic theory?

3. Briefly discuss the PNB auction of certificates of deposit in terms of the consumer. Are consumers getting a good deal from electronic auctions or is this a marketing gimmick that only enhances the company auctioning off some good or service?

4. The article describes some elements that are associated with monopolistic competition. Explain what this is and how it fits into an analysis of these trends.

Part Seven
RISK, UNCERTAINTY, AND INCENTIVES

CHAPTER 13

Risk Analysis

Chapter Profile

Risk is a hazard or a chance of a loss. The probability of a particular outcome is the proportion of times that this outcome occurs over the long run if this situation exists over and over again. **Expected profit** is the sum of the amount of money gained (or lost) if each outcome occurs times the probability of occurrence of the outcome.

A **decision tree** represents a decision problem as a series of choices, each of which is depicted by a **decision fork** or a chance fork. A decision tree can be used to determine the course of action with the highest expected monetary value. As an example, we took up the decision of whether or not to drill an oil well.

The expected value of perfect information is the increase in expected monetary value if the decision maker could obtain completely accurate information concerning the outcome of the relevant situation (but he or she does not yet know what this information will be). This is the maximum amount that the decision maker should pay to obtain such information. Using methods described in this chapter, one can calculate the expected value of perfect information.

Risk is often measured by the standard deviation or coefficient of variation of the **probability distribution** of profit. Whether a decision maker wants to maximize expected profit depends on his or her attitudes toward risk. The decision maker's attitudes toward risk can be measured by his or her utility function.

To construct such a utility function, we begin by setting the utility attached to two monetary values arbitrarily. Then we present the decision maker with a choice between the certainty of one of the other monetary values and a gamble where the possible outcomes are the two monetary values whose utilities we set arbitrarily. Repeating this procedure over and over, we can construct the decision maker's utility function.

One way to adjust the basic valuation model for risk is to use certainty equivalents in place of the expected profit figures in the equations in the next section. Based on the decision maker's utility function, one may be able to construct indifference curves showing the certainty equivalent corresponding to each uncertain outcome.

Another way to introduce risk into the valuation model is to adjust the discount rate. Based on the decision maker's utility function, one may be able to construct indifference curves between expected rate of return and risk. Using such indifference curves, one can estimate the risk premium (if any) that is appropriate.

Key Formulas to Remember

1. Expected profit:

$$E(\pi) = \sum_{i-1}^{N} \pi P_i$$

where π_1 is the level of profit associated with the ith outcome, P is the probability that the ith outcome will take place, and N is the number of possible outcomes.

2. Standard deviation:

$$\sigma = \left(\sum_{i-1}^{N} P_i \left[\pi_i - E(\pi) \right]^2 \right)^{0.5}$$

where σ is the standard deviation.

3. Coefficient of variation:

$$V = \left(\frac{\sigma}{E(\pi)} \right)$$

where V is the coefficient of variation.

Questions

Completion

1. If a decision maker's utility function is _____, the decision maker maximizes expected monetary value.

2. The Millrose Company stores spare parts at two warehouses, one in Scranton and one in Cleveland. The number of defective and acceptable spare parts at each warehouse is as follows.

	Number of spare parts		
Warehouse	*Defective*	*Acceptable*	*Total*
Scranton	200	800	1,000
Cleveland	50	450	500

If one of the 1,500 spare parts kept by the firm is chosen at random (i.e., if each spare part has a 1/1,500 chance of being chosen), the probability that it will be defective is _____.

3. In the previous question, the probability that the chosen spare part will be at the Scranton warehouse is _____.

4. In question 2, the probability that the chosen spare part will be *both* defective and at the Scranton warehouse is _____.

5. In calculating the expected value of perfect information, it is important to recognize that the decision maker (does, does not) _____ know what this information will be.

6. When a decision maker applies the maximin rule, he or she assumes that nature (or whatever force determines the outcome of the situation) dictates that, if any course of action is taken, the _____ outcome will occur.

7. Whether a decision maker wants to maximize expected profit depends on his or her attitude toward _____.

8. A(n) _____ fork is a juncture representing a choice where the decision maker is in control of the outcome.

9. A(n) _____ fork is a juncture where "chance" controls the outcome.

10. If the decision maker's utility function is linear, he or she (will, will not) _____ maximize expected profit.

True or False

_____ 1. The maximization of expected utility results in the same decisions as the maximin rule if the utility function is linear.

_____ 2. Under conditions of uncertainty, it is easy to formulate optimal general rules for decision makers; they should maximize expected utility, using the known probabilities of the relevant outcomes.

_____ 3. Risk and uncertainty are indistinguishable.

_____ 4. According to the subjective definition of probability, the probability of a particular outcome is the proportion of times that this outcome occurs over the long run if this situation exists over and over again.

_____ 5. One problem with the maximin rule is that it ignores the maximum amount that the decision makers can lose.

_____ 6. If James Johnson is indifferent between the certainty of a $50,000 gain and a gamble where there is a 0.4 probability of a $40,000 gain and a 0.6 probability of a $60,000 gain, the utility he attaches to a $50,000 gain equals $0.4U(40) + 0.6U(60)$, where $U(40)$ is the utility he attaches to a $40,000 gain, and $U(60)$ is the utility he attaches to a $60,000 gain.

_____ 7. If a firm accepts a particular gamble, there is a 0.3 chance that it will gain $1 million and a 0.6 chance that it will lose $2 million. Based on this information, one cannot calculate the expected monetary value of this gamble to the firm.

_____ 8. If John Jeffries is a risk averter, his utility function is linear.

_____ 9. If Mary Solomon is a risk lover, her utility function is linear.

_____ 10. Martin Bush is willing to accept greater risks only if he obtains a higher expected rate of return. Thus, he is a risk averter.

Multiple Choice

1. If a decision maker is indifferent to risk, and if the expected value of perfect information is $40,000, the decision maker should be willing to pay the following for perfect information:

   a. $35,000
   b. $45,000
   c. $55,000
   d. $65,000
   e. $75,000

2. If a decision maker is a risk averter for values of monetary gain above $10,000, then he or she:

   a. must be a risk averter for values of monetary gain below $10,000
   b. must be risk neutral for values of monetary gain below $10,000
   c. must be a risk lover for values of monetary gain below $10,000
   d. must be either a or b
   e. none of the above

3. William Moran rolls a true die. If the die comes up a 2, he receives $6,000; if it does not come up a 2, he pays $1,000. The expected monetary value of this gamble to him is:

   a. $1,167
   b. $833
   c. $167
   d. −$167
   e. −$833

4. William Moran's utility function is $U = 10 + 3M$, where U is utility, and M is monetary gain (in dollars). He will prefer the certainty of a gain of $20 over a gamble where there is a 0.3 probability of a $9 gain and a 0.7 probability of:

   a. a $31 gain
   b. a $29 gain
   c. a $27 gain
   d. a $25 gain
   e. none of the above

5. In the previous question, if William Moran has a 0.4 probability of receiving $100 and a 0.6 probability of losing $200, the expected utility of this gamble is:

   a. −70
   b. −80
   c. −230
   d. −250
   e. none of the above

6. The difference between the expected rate of return on a specific risky investment and that on a riskless investment is called:

a. the risk-adjusted discount rate
b. the risk premium on this investment
c. the investment's level of risk
d. all of the above
e. none of the above

Problems

1. The Deming Company must determine whether or not to add a new product line. If the new product line is a success, the firm will increase its profits by $1 million; if it is not a success, its profits will decrease by $0.5 million. Deming's managers feel that the probability is 0.6 that the new product line will be a success and 0.4 that it will not be a success.

   a. If Deming's managers are risk neutral, should they add the new product line?
   b. How would you determine whether they are risk neutral?
   c. What is the expected value of perfect information to them?

2. A newspaper publisher in a small town must decide whether or not to publish a Sunday edition. The publisher thinks that the probability is 0.7 that a Sunday edition would be a success and 0.3 that it would be a failure. If it is a success, he will gain $200,000. If it is a failure, he will lose $100,000.

   a. Construct the decision tree for this problem, and use it to solve the problem, assuming that the publisher is risk neutral.
   b. What is the expected value of perfect information?
   c. How would you go about trying to determine whether the publisher is in fact risk neutral?

3. A Tucson restaurant owner must decide whether or not to expand his restaurant. He thinks that the probability is 0.6 that the expansion will prove successful and 0.4 that it will not be successful. If it is successful, he will gain $100,000. If it is not successful, he will lose $80,000.

   a. Construct the decision tree for this problem, and use it to solve the problem, assuming that the restaurant owner is risk neutral.
   b. List all forks in the decision tree you constructed, indicate whether each is a decision fork or a chance fork, and state why.

4. In the previous problem, would the restaurant owner's decision be altered if he felt that:

   a. the probability that the expansion will prove successful is 0.5, not 0.6?
   b. the probability that the expansion will prove successful is 0.7, not 0.6?
   c. What value of the probability that the expansion will prove successful will make the restaurant owner indifferent between expanding and not expanding the restaurant?

5. The president of the Hawaii Company says that she is indifferent between the certainty of receiving $100,000 and a gamble where there is a 0.5 chance of receiving $250,000 and a 0.5 chance of receiving nothing. In the following graph, plot three points on her utility function.

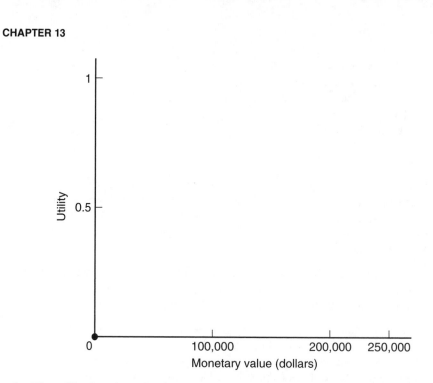

6. The utility function of the president of the Manhattan Company follows.

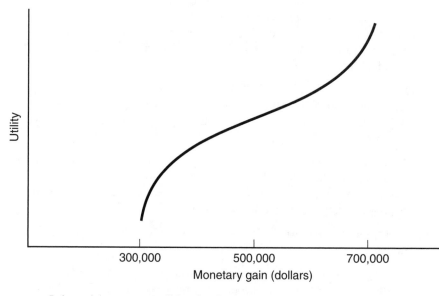

a. Is he a risk averter at all levels of monetary gain?
b. Is he a risk lover at all levels of monetary gain?
c. Does he prefer the certainty of gaining $400,000 over a gamble where there is a 0.5 probability of gaining $300,000 and a 0.5 probability of gaining $500,000?

7. If each card in a standard 52-card deck of playing cards has the same probability of being drawn, what is the probability that a single card that is drawn will be:

   a. a red 9?
   b. a black ace?
   c. a black card?
   d. neither a red card nor a queen?
   e. a queen, king, or ace?

8. a. The Rosetree Corporation is considering the purchase of a firm that produces tools and dies. Rosetree's management feels that there is a 50–50 chance, if Rosetree buys the firm, that it can make the firm into an effective producer of auto parts. If the firm can be transformed in this way, Rosetree believes that it will make $1 million if it buys the firm; if it cannot be transformed in this way, Rosetree believes that it will lose $2 million. What is the expected monetary value to Rosetree of buying the firm?
   b. In fact, the Rosetree Corporation decides to purchase the firm described in the previous question. Does this mean that Rosetree's management is risk neutral or risk averse?

9. The utility function of the president of the Howe Company can be represented by the following equation:

$$U = 10 + 2M$$

where U is utility, and M is monetary gain (in thousands of dollars). He has the opportunity to invest $25,000 in a small electronics firm. He believes there is a 0.5 probability that he will lose his entire investment and a 0.5 probability that he will gain $32,000.

   a. If he makes the investment, what is his expected utility?
   b. Should he make the investment?

10. An appliance firm must decide whether or not to offer Roland Whelan a job. If Whelan turns out to be a success, the firm will increase its profits by $100,000; if he turns out not to be a success, the firm's profits will decrease by $80,000. The firm feels that the chances are 50–50 that he will be a success.

    a. What is the expected value of perfect information?
    b. What is the expected monetary value to the firm if it does not hire Whelan?
    c. What is the expected monetary value to the firm if it hires Whelan?

11. A firm must decide whether or not to go forward with an R and D project to develop a new process. If the project is successful, it will gain $5 million; if it is not successful, it will lose $1 million. Suppose that the firm has no idea of what the probabilities of success or failure may be. If the maximin rule is applied, should the firm go forward with the R and D project? Why or why not?

12. a. The Contact Engineering Company must decide whether or not to buy a piece of equipment. If it buys this equipment, and if the price of ammonia increases by more than 10 percent in the next year, it will make $3 million; if it buys the equipment, and the price of ammonia does not increase by this amount in the next year, it will lose $2 million. If it does not buy the equipment, it gains (and loses) nothing, regardless of what happens to the price of ammonia. Construct

a table showing the firm's profits if each possible outcome occurs, given that the firm takes each possible course of action.

b. What decision should the Contact Engineering Company make, if it applies the maximin rule? What criticisms can be made of this rule?

13. William McCarthy's indifference curve between expected rate of return and risk follows:

a. For him, what is the risk premium for an investment where $\sigma = 3$?
b. If $\sigma = 2$, what is the risk-adjusted discount rate?
c. What is the riskless discount rate?

14. PB&J Corporation hopes to implement a new production technology next year. The probability of the technology being ready to implement by then equals 0.75, and it would increase profits by $2 million. If the technology is not implemented, the corporation expects to lose $600,000. What is the expected change in next year's profit for PB&J?

15. Cabal Inc. could increase its profits by $100,000 next year if it changes the work rules in its plant. However, if it does so, it faces a 20 percent chance of a labor action that could result in a loss of $600,000. What is the expected increase in profits to Cabal by changing its work rules?

Answers

Completion

1. linear   2. $250/1{,}500 = 1/6$ 3. $1{,}000/1{,}500 = 2/3$ 4. $200/1{,}500 = 2/15$
5. does not   6. worst   7. risk   8. decision   9. chance   10. will

True or False

1. False 2. False 3. False 4. False 5. False 6. True 7. True 8. False
9. False 10. True

Multiple Choice

1. a 2. e 3. c 4. e 5. c 6. b

Problems

1. a. Yes.
   b. Construct the utility function of the decision maker.
   c. $200,000

2. a.

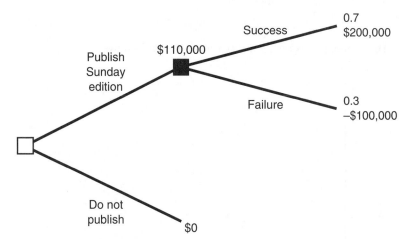

   He should publish the Sunday edition.
   b. 0.7($200,000) + 0.3(0) − $110,000 = $30,000
   c. Construct his utility function.

3. a.

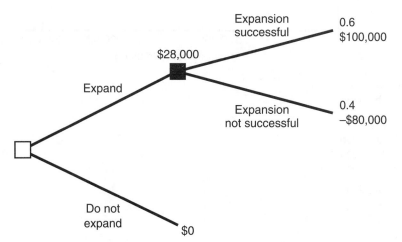

Since the expected monetary value if he expands is $0.6 (\$100,000) + 0.4 (-\$80,000) = \$28,000$, he should expand the restaurant.

b. The first fork on the left is a decision fork, since the restaurant owner decides whether or not to expand. The next fork is a chance fork, since "chance" decides whether or not the expansion is successful.

4. a. No.
   b. No.
   c. 4/9

5. Let zero be the utility of receiving nothing, and 1 be the utility of receiving $250,000. Then, since she is indifferent between the certainty of receiving $100,000 and the gamble described in the problem, the utility of receiving $100,000 must equal

$$0.5(1) + 0.5(0) = 0.5$$

Thus, three points on her utility function are as follows.

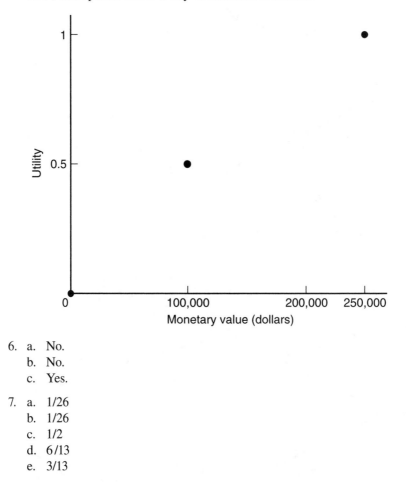

6. a. No.
   b. No.
   c. Yes.

7. a. 1/26
   b. 1/26
   c. 1/2
   d. 6/13
   e. 3/13

8. a. $0.5(\$1 \text{ million}) + 0.5(-2 \text{ million}) = -\$0.5 \text{ million}$
   b. Neither. It would have chosen not to purchase it if it were risk neutral, and it would have chosen not to purchase it if it were risk averse.

9. a. The utility of $-\$25,000$ equals $10 + 2(-25) = -40$. The utility of $+\$32,000$ equals $10 + 2(32) = 74$. His expected utility equals $0.5(-40) + 0.5(74) = 17$.
   b. Since the expected utility if he makes the investment (17) exceeds the expected utility if he does not make it (10), he should make it.

10. a. $0.5(\$100,000) + 0.5(0) - \$10,000 = \$40,000$
    b. zero
    c. $0.5(\$100,000) + 0.5(-\$80,000) = \$10,000$

11. No, because the maximum loss if it goes ahead with the project is $1 million, whereas the maximum loss if it does not go ahead with it is zero.

12. a.

	Price of ammonia increases by more than 10%	Price of ammonia increases by 10% or less
	(Profits of Contact Engineering Company)	
Contact buys equipment	+$3 million	−$2 million
Contact does not buy equipment	zero	zero

   b. It should not buy the equipment. It assumes that the worse outcome will occur, if each action is taken. This may be far too pessimistic.

13. a. 8 percent
    b. 10 percent
    c. 7 percent

14. $\$1,350,000 = 0.75 \cdot (\$2,000,000) + 0.25 \cdot (-\$600,000)$

15. $-\$40,000 = 0.8 \cdot (\$100,000) + 0.20 \cdot (-\$600,000)$

CHAPTER 14

Principal–Agent Issues and Managerial Compensation

Chapter Profile

The principal–agent problem arises from conflicting incentives and from the separation of ownership and control within a firm. **Moral hazard** is a variant of this problem and arises with third-party payer models, typically those involving insurers.

While owners of a firm wish to maximize the value of their shares, the managers of the firm may wish to minimize effort, enhance job security, and maximize pay. This chapter covers these types of inconsistent incentives faced by owners and managers and their possible resolution.

The situation of **incentive conflict** is further complicated by the facts that owners can neither directly observe a manager's level of effort nor can profits be used as an indicator of performance in a risky environment. Although a flat salary can be paid to a manager, given that effort imposes a cost on managers, it follows that under this compensation scheme the manager may provide the least amount of acceptable effort.

Consequently, incentive-compatible contracts should be designed to align the manager's interests with those of the owners of the firm—profit maximization. Such incentive-compatible contracts typically focus on awarding a bonus to the manager, which takes the form of a percentage of a firm's profit.

It should be noted that, given the higher relative level of risk aversion of managers to owners, the costs of these bonuses will exceed the dollar amount of the flat salary. The return to these compensation schemes, however, lies in the increased level of profit of the firm from increased effort on the manager's part.

The principal agent also extends beyond the firm. The chapter closes with discussions that focus on product liability and consumer protection, and it outlines some of the arguments for and against the need for safety regulation of consumer goods. Additionally, the potential conflict between creditors and owners is highlighted through the presentation of the **asset-substitution problem**, which can lead to the inability of a firm to obtain credit for profitable undertakings.

Questions

Completion

1. Owners are concerned with the value of their _____.

2. Owners are _____ risk averse than managers.

3. The principal–agent problem is one in which _____ cannot be monitored.

4. Principal–agent problems arise from _____ incentives.

5. Principal–agent problems that arise are sometimes referred to as problems of _____.

6. The objective of managers is to maximize their _____.

7. Contracts that allow owners and managers to share in the profits of the firm are called _____ contracts.

8. The expression "There is a trade-off between risk sharing and efficiency" summarizes principal–agent problems that involve _____.

9. Executive compensation is usually designed around two competing ideas: _____ and _____.

10. The price at which the stock can be purchased under a stock option plan is called the _____ or _____ price.

11. In insurance, the principal–agent problem is called _____.

12. The reluctance of policyholders (who have suffered some misfortune) to keep the cost of the event under control is called _____ moral hazard.

True or False

_____ 1. When the interests of the principal and agent are identical, principal–agent problems do not arise.

_____ 2. All else being equal, managers can be expected to be more risk averse than owners.

_____ 3. The reason that managers are more risk averse than owners is because owners can diversify their portfolio (wealth), whereas managers rely on their managerial income.

_____ 4. Under a flat salary compensation scheme, the manager is better off providing as little effort as possible.

_____ 5. Without any risk, you can infer the level of effort from a firm's profit.

_____ 6. The striking price is fixed under an indexed option.

_____ 7. Ex–post moral hazard refers to the tendency of policyholders to take less care to prevent future losses when they have insurance.

_____ 8. The par value of a bond is the same as the face value or principal amount of the bond.

_____ 9. Product liability laws are necessary to align the interests of consumers and producers.

_____ 10. The real nature of the principal–agent problem is that, when effort is not observable by the principal, it cannot be rewarded or penalized directly.

Multiple Choice

1. Which of the following are plausible objectives of a firm's managers?

    a. minimizing effort
    b. maximizing job security
    c. maximizing pay
    d. avoiding failure
    e. all of the above

2. The value of a call option is inversely related to:

    a. the strike price of a stock
    b. the current stock price
    c. market volatility
    d. firm revenue
    e. none of the above

3. Which of the following is not a potential solution to the asset-substitution problem?

    a. funding with equity
    b. establishing a reputation for protecting creditors
    c. precommitting to insure risk
    d. subjugating earlier debt
    e. none of the above

4. Which of the following is not an underlying issue of principal–agent problems?

    a. There is separation of ownership and control.
    b. The manager's effort is not observable.
    c. All else being equal, owners are more risk averse than managers.
    d. Business risks exist beyond the manager's control.
    e. none of the above

5. Which of the following is a factor in setting managerial compensation?

    a. the level of risk sharing
    b. meeting efficiency criteria
    c. the prevailing market wage for managers
    d. the current stock price
    e. all of the above

6. Indexed stock options:

    a. more closely identify a manager's level of effort
    b. reduce the cost of incentive-compatible contracts
    c. are worth more in a "bull" market
    d. are worth more to managers than nonindexed options
    e. none of the above

Problems

1. Assume that PB&J Corporation operates in a riskless endeavor and that shareholders can observe the amount of effort expended by their management. Further assume that PB&J's weekly revenue function is captured by $R(e) = 5,000 + 72e^{0.5}$, and the manager's disutility of effort by $u(e) = 750 + 6e$. Moreover, the firm faces weekly production costs of $1,200, and the manager will not work for PB&J unless she receives a net benefit of $1,470 per week.

    a. How much effort will the manager provide per week (expressed in weekly hours)?
    b. What is PB&J's weekly profit?
    c. What percentage of profit will PB&J pay to its manager?

2. Assume that Goshanski Inc., a hair replacement company, operates a riskless endeavor and that it can observe the amount of effort expended by its management. Further assume that Goshanski's weekly revenue function is captured by $R(e) = 4,500 + 40e^{0.75}$, and the CEO's disutility of effort by $u(e) = 750 + 12e$. Moreover, the firm faces weekly production costs of $1,700, and the CEO will not work for Goshanski unless he receives a net benefit of $1,100 per week.

    a. How much effort will the manager provide per week (expressed in weekly hours)?
    b. What is Goshanski's weekly profit?
    c. What percentage of profit will Goshanski pay to its CEO?

3. The equity value of Wiltgen Enterprises, an electronic equipment firm, equals $5,000,000 (probability of 0.5) or $15,000,000 (probability of 0.5). The firm's manager is risk averse and has a utility function of manager's utility = (compensation)$^{0.5}$, and the manager is assumed to receive all her wealth from the firm. To be competitive, the firm must offer the manager a compensation package with an expected utility of $1,500.

    a. What minimum flat salary must be paid to the manager to maintain her employment at Wiltgen Enterprises?
    b. What is the expected equity, after compensation, to the shareholders of Wiltgen Enterprises?
    c. What minimum percentage of equity must the manager be paid to maintain her employment at Wiltgen Enterprises?
    d. What is the expected equity remaining to shareholders after this form of compensation is paid?
    e. What is the dollar amount of the risk premium paid to the manager of Wiltgen Enterprises?

4. The equity value of RED Inc., a real estate development corporation, equals $5,000,000 (probability of 0.75) or $15,000,000 (probability of 0.25). The firm's manager is risk averse and has a utility function of manager's utility = (compensation)$^{0.5}$, and the manager is assumed to receive all her wealth from the firm. To be competitive, the firm must offer the manager a compensation package with an expected utility of $2,000.

    a. What percentage of equity must the manager be paid in order for her to maintain employment at RED Inc.?

b. What is the expected equity remaining to shareholders after this form of compensation is paid?

c. What is the dollar amount of the risk premium paid to the manager?

5. The following payoff table summarizes gross profits (before compensation) arising from two different levels of effort and factors outside of the manager's control (stage of the business cycle and resulting sales).

	Gross profits	
	Recession	*Expansion*
	Probability = 0.5	Probability = 0.5
Low effort	$75,000	$200,000
High effort	$150,000	$400,000

Assume that the disutility of "high" effort is 50 for the manager and that he or she is risk averse, so that utility $= (\text{compensation})^{0.5}$.

a. What is the expected gross profit of the firm after compensation if the manager is paid a flat salary of $40,000?

b. What bonus (percentage of gross profit) should be paid to the manager in lieu of this flat salary in order to maximize gross profit to the corporation after compensation?

c. What is the dollar amount of expected gross profit after the appropriate compensation bonus is paid to the manager?

6. The following payoff table summarizes gross profits (before compensation) arising from two different levels of effort and factors outside of the manager's control (stage of the business cycle and resulting sales).

	Gross profits	
	Increasing rates	*Constant rates*
	Probability = 0.25	Probability = 0.75
Low effort	$500,000	$1,000,000
High effort	$750,000	$3,000,000

Assume that the disutility of "high" effort is 25 for the manager and that he or she is risk averse, so that utility $= (\text{compensation})^{0.5}$.

a. What is the expected gross profit of the firm after compensation if the manager is paid a flat salary of $75,000?

b. What bonus (percentage of gross profit) should be paid to the manager in lieu of this flat salary in order to maximize gross profit to the corporation after compensation?

c. What is the dollar amount of expected gross profit after the appropriate compensation bonus is paid to the manager?

7. Assume that home owners who finance their homes are required by the lender to carry fire insurance and that statistical studies show that such home owners face a 1-in-100 chance of suffering from a fire annually. Further studies have documented that when smoke detectors are installed (at a cost of $400) the average losses arising from a fire fall from $75,000 to $25,000. Further, assume that the average home value is $100,000 and the home owners' utility function takes the form $U = W^{0.5}$.

a. Would home owners install fire detectors if no insurance was available?
b. If the insurance company designs a policy charging $1,000 annually, will home owners install fire detectors in their homes?
c. Would such a policy be profitable for the insurance company? Could this premium be maintained in a competitive market?
d. What premium would be charged in a competitive market?

8. Assume that home owners who finance their homes are required by the lender to carry fire insurance, and that statistical studies show that such home owners face a 1-in-100 chance of suffering from a fire annually. Further studies have documented that when smoke detectors are installed (at a cost of $300), the average losses arising from a fire fall from $100,000 to $25,000. Further, assume that the average home value is $100,000, and the home owners' utility function takes the form $U = W^{0.5}$.

a. PDQ Insurance Corporation offers a policy with a 30 percent home owner copayment for damages with a premium of $125. Will home owners install fire detectors?
b. Would such a policy be profitable for the insurance company? What premium would be charged in a competitive market?
c. What percentage of the copayment would the insurance company have to implement for these policies to break even?

Answers

Completion

1. shares   2. less   3. effort   4. conflicting   5. moral hazard   6. net benefit of employment   7. incentive-compatible   8. risk   9. risk sharing, efficiency   10. striking, exercise   11. moral hazard   12. ex-post

True or False

1. True   2. True   3. True   4. True   5. True   6. False   7. False   8. True   9. False   10. True

Multiple Choice

1. e   2. a   3. d   4. c   5. e   6. c

Problems

1. a. $\pi(e) = R(e) - u(e) - C$

$$\pi(e) = 5,000 + 72e^{0.5} - (750 + 6e) - 1,200$$
$$\pi(e) = 3,050 + 72e^{0.5} - 6e$$
$$\text{Max}_e\ 3,050 + 72e^{0.5} - 6e$$

FOC

$$e:\ 36e^{-0.5} - 6 = 0$$
$$e = 36\ (\text{hours per week})$$

Alternatively, since the manager will equate the marginal benefit of effort to its marginal cost,

$$\frac{\Delta R(e)}{\Delta e} = \frac{\Delta u(e)}{\Delta e}$$

$$0.5 \cdot 72e^{0.5-1} = 6$$

$$e^{-0.5} = \frac{6}{36}$$

$$e^{0.5} = \frac{36}{6}$$

$$e = (6)^2$$
$$e = 36$$

b. $\pi(e) = 3{,}050 + 72e^{0.5} - 6e$

$e = 3{,}266$

c. $\alpha = \dfrac{1{,}470}{3{,}266}$

$\alpha = 0.45$

2. a. $\pi(e) = R(e) - u(e) - C$

$\pi(e) = 4{,}500 + 40e^{0.75} - (750 + 12e) - 1{,}700$
$\pi(e) = 2{,}050 + 40e^{0.75} - 12e$
$\text{Max}_e\ 2{,}050 + 40e^{0.75} - 12e$

FOC

$e:\ 30e^{-0.25} - 12 = 0$
$e = 39$ (hours per week)

Alternatively, since the manager will equate the marginal benefit of effort to its marginal cost,

$$\frac{\Delta R(e)}{\Delta e} = \frac{\Delta u(e)}{\Delta e}$$

$$0.75 \cdot 40e^{0.75-1} = 12$$

$$e^{-0.25} = \frac{12}{30}$$

$$e^{0.25} = \frac{30}{12}$$

$$e = (2.5)^4$$
$$e = 39$$

b. $\pi(e) = 2{,}050 + 40e^{0.75} - 12e$

$e = 2{,}206.25$

c. $\alpha = \dfrac{1{,}100}{2{,}206.25}$

$\alpha = 0.4986$

3. a. $1,500 = (\text{Compensation})^{0.5}$

$\text{Compensation} = (1,500)^2$
$\text{Compensation} = \$2,250,000$

b. Equity before compensation:

$\text{EQUITY}_{\text{before comp}} = \$5,000,000 \text{ (probability of } 0.5\text{) or}$
$\qquad\qquad\qquad\qquad 15,000,000 \text{ (probability of } 0.5\text{)}$
$\text{EQUITY}_{\text{before comp}} = \$2,250,000 + \$7,500,000$
$\text{EQUITY}_{\text{before comp}} = \$1,000,000$

The answer to part a above indicates compensation should be $2,250,000, so that:

$\text{EQUITY}_{\text{after comp}} = \text{EQUITY}_{\text{before comp}} - \text{Compensation}$
$\text{EQUITY}_{\text{after comp}} = \$10,000,000 - \$2,250,000$
$\text{EQUITY}_{\text{after comp}} = \$7,750,000$

c. $1,500 = 0.5\sqrt{5,000,000x} + 0.5\sqrt{15,000,000x}$

$3,000 = 2,236.07\sqrt{x} + 3,872.98\sqrt{x}$

$3,000 = 6,109.05\sqrt{x}$

$x^{0.5} = \dfrac{3,000}{6,109.05}$

$x = 0.572025$

d. First, figure out the compensation paid to the manager:

$\text{Compensation} = 0.2411543 \cdot \$10,000,000$
$\text{Compensation} = \$2,411,543$

So, remaining equity equals:

$\text{EQUITY}_{\text{after comp}} = \$10,000,000 - \$2,411,543$
$\text{EQUITY}_{\text{after comp}} = \$7,588,457$

The risk premium is the difference in what is paid under the two schemes.

$\text{Risk premium} = \$2,411,543 - \$2,250,000$
$\text{Risk premium} = \$161,543$

4. a. $2,000 = 0.75\sqrt{5,000,000x} + 0.25\sqrt{15,000,000x}$

$2,000 = 1,677.0509\sqrt{x} + 968.24582\sqrt{x}$

$2,000 = 2,645.2967\sqrt{x}$

$x^{0.5} = \dfrac{2,000}{2,645.2967}$

$x = 0.572025$

b. Equity before compensation:

$\text{EQUITY}_{\text{before comp}} = \$5,000,000 \text{ (probability of } 0.75\text{) or}$
$\qquad\qquad\qquad\qquad \$15,000,000 \text{ (probability of } 0.25\text{)}$
$\text{EQUITY}_{\text{before comp}} = \$3,750,000 + \$3,750,000$
$\text{EQUITY}_{\text{before comp}} = \$7,500,000$

Compensation is:

$$\text{Compensation} = 0.572025 \cdot \$7,500,000$$
$$\text{Compensation} = \$4,290,187.50$$

Therefore,

$$\text{EQUITY}_{\text{after comp}} = \text{EQUITY}_{\text{before comp}} - \text{compensation}$$
$$\text{EQUITY}_{\text{after comp}} = \$7,750,000 - \$4,290,188$$
$$\text{EQUITY}_{\text{after comp}} = \$3,459,812$$

   c. The risk premium is the difference in what is paid under the two schemes. Under a flat salary, compensation would have been

$$2,000 = (\text{compensation})^{0.5}$$
$$\text{Compensation} = \$4,000,000$$
$$\text{Risk premium} = \$4,290,187.50 - \$4,000,000$$
$$\text{Risk premium} = \$290,187.50$$

5. a. First, note that a flat salary of $40,000 will lead the manager to pursue the low-effort path as

$$\text{Utility low effort} = (40,000)^{0.5} = 200$$
$$\text{Utility high effort} = (40,000)^{0.5} - 50 = 150$$

The manager will clearly pursue the low-effort path, which implies that

$$\text{Expected profit}_{\text{low effort}} = 0.5 \cdot 75,000 + 0.5 \cdot 20,000 - 40,000$$
$$\text{Expected profit}_{\text{low effort}} = \$97,500$$

   b. Utility low effort (flat salary) = expected utility high effort (with bonus)

$$200 = 0.5\sqrt{150,000x} + 0.5\sqrt{400,000x} - 50$$
$$500 = 1019.8\sqrt{x}$$
$$x = 0.24$$

So the bonus equals

$$\text{Bonus} = 0.24 \cdot (0.5 \cdot 150,000 + 0.5 \cdot 400,000)$$
$$\text{Bonus} = 1019.8\sqrt{x}$$
$$\text{Bonus} = \$66,000$$

   c. $\text{Profit} = \$275,000 - \$66,000$

$$\text{Profit} = \$209,000$$

But be sure to verify that the manager is better off providing high effort with the bonus:

Expected utility low effort with bonus

$$= 0.5 \cdot (0.24 \cdot 75,000)^{0.5} + 0.5 \cdot (0.24 \cdot 200,000)^{0.5}$$
$$= 176.16$$

Expected utility high effort with bonus

$$= 0.5 \cdot (0.24 \cdot 150,000)^{0.5} + 0.5 \cdot (0.24 \cdot 400,000)^{0.5} - 50$$
$$= 200$$

6. a. First, note that a flat salary of $75,000 will lead the manager to pursue the low effort path as

Utility low effort $= (75,000)^{0.5} = 273.86$
Utility high effort $= (75,000)^{0.5} - 25 = 248.86$

The manager will clearly pursue the low-effort path, which implies that

Expected profit$_{\text{low effort}} = 0.25 \cdot 500,000 + 0.75 \cdot 1,000,000 - 75,000$
Expected profit$_{\text{low effort}} = \$800,000$

b. Utility low effort (flat salary) = expected utility high effort (with bonus)

$273.86 = 0.25\sqrt{750,000x} + 0.75\sqrt{3,000,000x} - 25$
$298.86 = 1,515.5\sqrt{x}$
$x = 0.039$

So the bonus equals

Bonus $= 0.039 \cdot (0.25 \cdot 750,000 + 0.75 \cdot 3,000,000)$
Bonus $= 0.039 \cdot \$2,437,500$
Bonus $= \$95,063$

c. Profit $= \$2,437,500 - \$95,063$

Profit $= \$2,342,438$

But be sure to verify that the manager is better off providing high effort with the bonus:
Expected utility low effort with bonus

$= 0.25 \cdot (0.039 \cdot 500,000)^{0.5} + 0.75 \cdot (0.039 \cdot 3,000,000)^{0.5}$
$= 183.02$

Expected utility high effort with bonus

$= 0.25 \cdot (0.039 \cdot 750,000)^{0.5} + 0.75 \cdot (0.039 \cdot 3,000,000)^{0.5} - 25$
$= 274$

7. a. Yes, compare their respective utility levels with and without fire detectors.

Utility = (home value – cost of fire detector – expected loss due to fire)$^{0.5}$

So that

UTILITY$_{\text{no detector}} = (100,000 - 0 - 0.01 \cdot 75,000)^{0.5}$
UTILITY$_{\text{no detector}} = 315.04$
UTILITY$_{\text{detector}} = (100,000 - 400 - 0.01 \cdot 25,000)^{0.5}$
UTILITY$_{\text{detector}} = 315.52$

b. No.

Utility = (Home value – cost of fire detector – premium
    – expected loss due to fire)$^{0.5}$

$$\text{UTILITY}_{\text{no detector}} = (100{,}000 - 0 - 1{,}000 - 0)^{0.5}$$
$$\text{UTILITY}_{\text{no detector}} = 314.64$$
$$\text{UTILITY}_{\text{detector}} = (100{,}000 - 400 - 1{,}000 - 0)^{0.5}$$
$$\text{UTILITY}_{\text{detector}} = 314.00$$

c. Expected loss is $750, since moral hazard exists and home owners will not install detectors. Given a premium of $1,000, the insurer realizes an average profit per policy of $250. This is not sustainable.

d. At break-even with this type of policy the premium should be $750.

8. a. No. Compare the respective levels of home owner utility:

Utility = (home value – cost of fire detector – premium –
   expected loss due to fire)$^{0.5}$
$$\text{UTILITY}_{\text{no detector}} = (100{,}000 - 0 - 150 - 0.01 \bullet 100{,}000 \bullet 0.3)^{0.5}$$
$$\text{UTILITY}_{\text{no detector}} = 315.36$$
$$\text{UTILITY}_{\text{detector}} = (100{,}000 - 300 - 150 - 0.01 \bullet 25{,}000 \bullet 0.3)^{0.5}$$
$$\text{UTILITY}_{\text{detector}} = 315.40$$

b. On average, fire detectors would not be installed, so the expected loss to the insurance company is $700. The expected profit is the premium less the expected loss, leaving a net profit of negative $550 per policy on average.

c. Just over 40 percent.

CHAPTER 15

Adverse Selection

Chapter Profile

Differences in the amount of knowledge and information each party to a business transaction may have are often large. We term these differences *asymmetric information,* and the asymmetry can lead to **adverse selection** or, in other words, an outcome where the uninformed party is at a disadvantage. In economic terms, these are imperfections of the market and can lead to subsidies and even to a market collapsing.

Remedies to this problem can be as simple as providing information to the parties involved or providing incentives for the disadvantage party to obtain information. Or, they can be more complex, involving contractual and financial arrangements that lead the parties that may have otherwise been disadvantaged in the transaction to make more informed decisions. For example, producers may use warranties to distinguish their products from rivals. Auto insurance companies may offer cheaper partial coverage to drivers with good records so they will not have to subsidize accident-prone drivers. Game theory, as well as many other tools of managerial economics, is useful in selecting the best methods for companies to overcome the issues of adverse selection.

Adverse selection is the lack of equal information among parties to a transaction before the transaction takes place. Moral hazard is the problem of a hidden action resulting from adverse selection. Both can lead to market failures.

Questions

Completion

1. In a market situation of buyers and sellers, adverse selection occurs when either the buyer or seller _____ information.

2. If banks cannot charge different interest rates (i.e., engage in price discrimination), then when interest rates increase, relatively good borrowers will (enter, leave) _____ the market and not take out loans, thus increasing the bank's default rate. (This assumes the borrower has a better knowledge of his or her risk than the bank.)

3. More information can actually make a market work (better, worse) _____ if it is asymmetrically distributed.

4. Adverse selection is the problem of unequal information _____ a transaction.

5. Moral hazard is a problem of _____ action after a transaction.

True or False

_____ 1. The Internet has eliminated the problem of asymmetric information.

_____ 2. Creating a separating equilibrium is the solution to the adverse selection problem.

_____ 3. Buyers of used cars are always at a knowledge disadvantage.

_____ 4. Adverse selection occurs when one party to a contractual relationship knows more than the other party or parties.

_____ 5. Good drivers have fewer accidents because they have few incentives to purchase insurance as a result of adverse selection problems.

Multiple Choice

1. In the labor market, employers who want to hire the best candidate for a job might avoid the problem of adverse selection by:

   a. asking candidates how much they expect to earn
   b. evaluating their educational background
   c. observing what type of car they drive
   d. testing their writing skills

2. In the insurance industry, the purchaser of insurance usually has:

   a. more information about his or her risk potential than the company
   b. less information about his or her risk potential than the company
   c. the same amount of information about his or her risk potential as the company

3. A separating equilibrium is inefficient since it is:

   a. sometimes difficult to achieve
   b. a cooperative effort of both parties to the transaction
   c. relatively expensive
   d. both b and c
   e. both a and c

4. A "signal" (as used in adverse selection) is:

   a. a message a seller sends to a buyer that is meant to confuse the buyer
   b. a lower price
   c. a message a seller sends to a buyer that conveys credible information
   d. deceptive advertising
   e. a message a buyer sends to a seller

5. Adverse selection is less of a problem in markets where:

   a. buyers and sellers have easy Internet access and accurate information is available on Web sites
   b. information is hidden and available only to those who subscribe to expensive trade publications

c. products are not standardized
d. there are many participants
e. television and radio advertising is used to convey information

Problems

1. All the residents of Baycity, a town of 1,000 people, own boats. Every year, each resident sells his or her used boat and purchases a new one. The old boats are of varying quality, and the owners are fully aware of how good or bad their boats are, but the buyers are ignorant of this information. Thus, each boat has an expected price, S, which reflects its true value. In 2005, the prices, S, will range between $0 and $4,000, and the number of boats worth less than S is $S/2$. The local boat-yard has a reputation for being honest and will evaluate the condition of a boat for a price of $500.

    a. If no seller were willing to spend $500 to have his or her boat evaluated, what would be the market price for a boat?
    b. If all boats worth more than Z were evaluated and all boats worth less than Z were not (under the assumption that the owners of high-quality used boats were willing to spend the $500, and the other owners were not), what would the market price for unevaluated boats be?
    c. In an equilibrium condition, one boat will be in the middle of the pack, where all boats in better condition will be evaluated and all boats in worse condition will not be. What will the value of that boat be?
    d. What will be the price of unevaluated boats in this market?

2. Asymmetric information can easily lead to an adverse selection problem. This is a common problem for many industries and sectors, since there are very few situations where all parties to a transaction have exactly the same information and knowledge. Discuss the role of government versus the role of firms themselves in creating solutions to these problems so that all parties can be better informed and make better decisions.

3. Discuss adverse selection in the case of workers' compensation insurance. Does a firm offering workers' compensation (assume the firm is unregulated and has a choice) provide incentives for workers to injure themselves?

4. In the used car market, discuss the mechanisms that can be used to alleviate the problem of adverse selection.

5. Suppose the Goodstitch clothing firm needs to hire supervisors, and there are two types, in equal proportions: high productivity employees (HPEs) with a marginal revenue product (MRP) of $200 and lower productivity employees (LPEs) with an MRP of $160. If the firm does not know what type any individual is, the firm would use an expected MRP of $180. The HPEs would like to signal the firm that they are worth more. Suppose the firm says it will pay a wage of $200 to anyone with a college degree, and HPEs could earn that degree more easily than LPEs. If you do not have the degree, the firm will pay you only $160. The degree adds nothing to a supervisor's productivity.

    Assume the cost to get a degree (in terms of time and effort, books, tuition) is $60 for the HPEs but $100 for the LPEs. Then, what will the equilibrium be? Will HPEs get the degree?

Answers

Completion

1. lacks the same 2. leave 3. worse 4. before 5. hidden

True or False

1. False 2. True 3. False 4. True 5. False

Multiple Choice

1. b 2. a 3. e 4. c 5. a

Problems

1. a. $2,000
   b. $Z/2$
   c. Solve $Z/2 = Z - \$500$, $Z = \$1,000$.
   d. $500

2. The insurance industry is a good example where firms have demonstrated that offering the same type of insurance with different coverage at different prices (e.g., deductibles for collision insurance) can provide incentives for good drivers to estimate their expected losses and purchase insurance without subsidizing poor drivers (or at least minimizing the subsidy). If there were no market solution to the problem, and if governments decided that driving without insurance is illegal, it would be up to the government to force insurance companies and drivers to both offer and purchase insurance, even if subsidies were involved. What usually occurs is a combination of governments requiring drivers to have insurance and companies finding methods for charging customers rates that allow good drivers to pay less (thus they are willing to purchase insurance), while forcing drivers with bad records to pay more.

   In a situation where governments are not involved, such as within a firm that has no easy way to distinguish between highly productive workers and those who are not as productive, it may be up to the employees themselves to provide better information to management. Otherwise, management would be forced into an adverse selection situation, where all employees would be paid the same, regardless of their individual productivity. As with all similar cases, the focus is on removing barriers to obtaining better information. Where employees might fear retaliation from revealing such information, other solutions exist, such as the firm itself offering incentives for better performance and allowing workers to choose jobs either where those incentives exist or are absent, thus creating a separating equilibrium.

3. Workers' compensation provides payment when employees are not able to work due to on-the-job injuries. Clearly, there may be an issue of adverse selection, since some will have the incentive to either injure themselves or fake injuries to avoid working while still getting paid. It is also difficult for a firm to know in advance which workers might be tempted to take advantage of this situation and hire only diligent workers. Solutions to this problem can be created through various methods, including limiting the payouts, limiting the time payouts can be collected, establishing a waiting period before the insurance will pay, and so forth. If, in reality, laws limit a firm's ability to affect payments from this type

of insurance, the firm can provide incentives such as increasing safety programs and safety inspections, or even imposing monetary penalties for violations of safety procedures to avoid injuries to workers.

4. Various effective methods include developing a good reputation for quality and developing standards (e.g., establishing a large national chain of used car dealerships with a reputation for honest business practices), providing guarantees and warranties on the product, providing more information, allowing inspections of cars prior to selling, having a government mandate purchase or return options for lemons, and using market signaling through truthful advertising.

5. Without the degree all workers will get $160, but with the degree they get $200 – $60, or $140. Therefore, the HPEs will get the degree. The LPEs will not get the degree since they will receive $160 without the degree, and with the degree they will get $160 – $100, or $60. Goodstitch has been successful in establishing a signaling equilibrium that separates the two types of employees. If the education had cost the LPEs only $20, this would not have worked. (Note that the education is wasteful—it added nothing to productivity—but it does help the market work better and enables Goodstitch to hire only those workers it wants.)

CASE SIX

The Carriage House Inn: A Family Corporation
Michael D. Everett

In the summer of 1987 Margot Filmore, a new generally trained MBA and consultant with a major bank and trust company in a large U.S. city, pondered her first assignment. What recommendations should she make to the heirs of The Carriage House Inn, Incorporated, a medium sized family corporation, which included a prosperous 70 room motel, six unit apartment building, and a residence converted into a small office building? She apparently faced two basic questions and some serious data problems. First, what constituted the best economic recommendations in terms of keeping or selling various segments of the corporation? Second, what recommendations would best fit the overall preferences of the heirs and keep peace in the family?

The lack of good managerial accounting and financial data for each segment of the corporation compounded the problem. The family corporation only had traditional financial report accounts, which lumped the three businesses, or segments, and fixed and variable costs together for tax reporting purposes (Exhibit 1). Although Margo could understand the output of commonly used accounting, financial, and statistical techniques, she would have to review some of them (Exhibit 2) and obtain help from

other staff members to develop appropriate models.

CORPORATE BACKGROUND

Through interviews with the surviving children Margo familiarized herself with the history of the family business and preferences of family members. In the early 1950s the Boyds with their four young children, Mary, Robert, Sally, and Jan, built a small stucco motel on a major commercial artery in the affluent, rapidly growing suburbs of a large U.S. city. The venture prospered with a 35-room one-story structure built in a U shape with a nicely landscaped courtyard. The business represented a total family. Mr. Boyd had the instincts and risk preferences for shrewd investments. Mrs. Boyd shared in the decision making and did most of the actual management of the motel, which they called the Carriage House Inn. The children and extended family helped in the physical labor from painting rooms to making beds.

By the mid 1950s the Carriage House Inn faced a major threat from a proposed interstate highway. This would shift traffic from a state highway, just half a mile from the motel, to an interchange about 3 miles away. Mr. Boyd joined with other local businesses in the area to fight the interstate, but lost. After it was completed, they were surprised to find that business actually improved.

Thus, gradually through the 1960s the family rebuilt the motel into a "modern," two-story brick structure which doubled its size to 70 rooms. The motel continued to prosper and generate substantial excess cash flow. For various reasons, including the desire to avoid marginal personal tax rates of over 50 percent, the Boyds incorporated and reinvested their excess profits into related businesses. First, they converted their old residence, which faced onto the major artery, into a small office building. Then they built a six-unit apartment building on an unused portion of the property facing a side street. As part of

their estate planning the parents placed the corporation into a trust for their children.

When Mr. Boyd passed away Mrs. Boyd continued to successfully manage the motel in cooperation with the estate trustees until her death in the mid 1980s. Robert and his wife, who lived in the area, took considerable interest in the motel and became involved in its management in the early 1980s. During Mrs. Boyd's final illness all the children took turns caring for her and managing the motel. After her death the children continued to cooperate and take turns managing the motel and other businesses. For Mary, Sally, and Jan this required traveling to the city every month and staying a week or more. Robert and his wife wanted to keep the motel and seriously considered quitting their jobs to manage it full time for the extended family.

EXHIBIT 1   Summary of the Carriage House Inn's Financial Report Accounts Projected for 1988 (Dollars/Year)

MOTEL INCOME	
Gross Motel Income	712,921.60
Bad Debts, Refunds, and Motel Tax	34,944.41
Motel Net Income	677,977.19
OTHER INCOME	
Office Building Income	23,426.00
Apartment Income	32,549.00
Total Other Income	55,975.00
GROSS CORPORATION INCOME	733,952.19
OPERATING EXPENSES	
Gross Payroll	197,245.82
Total Utilities	62,732.97
Total Services	98,436.72
Other Operating Expenses	26,421.40
Total General and Administrative	40,963.98
Depreciation	65,794.00
TOTAL CORPORATION EXPENSES	491,594.89
PRETAX CORPORATE INCOME	242,357.30
Federal Income Tax (.33)	79,977.91
State Income Tax (.08)	19,388.58
POST TAX INCOME	142,990.81

EXHIBIT 2   **Projected 1988 Managerial Cost and Cash Flow Accounts by Major Segment and for the Overall Corporation (Dollars/Year)**

	MOTEL	OFFICE	APT	OVERALL CORP
REVENUE	677,977	23,426	32,549	733,952
LESS VARIABLE	160,753	1,768	2,336	164,857
OPERATING CONTRIBUTION MARGIN	517,224	21,658	30,213	569,095
LESS UNDISTRIBUTED SEG COST	248,683	4,530	7,731	260,944
CONTRIBUTION TO FIXED COSTS	268,541	17,128	22,482	308,151
LESS FIXED COSTS				
DEPRECIATION	58,541	2,764	4,489	65,794
OPPORTUNITY COST OF ASSETS	204,000	22,000	30,000	256,000
EQUALS ASSETS IN SEGMENT	1,700,000	220,000	300,000	2,220,000
TIMES DISCOUNT RATE	0.12	0.10	0.10	0.115
NET SEGMENT MARGIN (NSM)	6,000	(7,636)	(12,007)	(13,643)
(Contribution to corp overhead and profits)				
FOR CASH FLOW ADD BACK IN				
OPPORTUNITY COST OF CAPITAL	204,000	22,000	30,000	256,000
TO NET SEGMENT MARGIN	6,000	(7,636)	(12,007)	(13,643)
EQUALS TAXABLE INCOME	210,000	14,364	17,993	242,357
LESS TAXES (.41)	86,100	5,889	7,377	99,367
PLUS DEPRECIATION	58,541	2,764	4,489	65,794
EQUALS NET CASH FLOW (CF)	182,441	11,239	15,105	208,785
CASH FLOW PAYOFF MEASURES				
NET MARKET VALUE OF ASSETS	1,700,000	220,000	300,000	2,220,000
ESTIMATED GROWTH OF ASSETS	0.00	0.00	0.00	0.00
(assume growth in land values equals depreciation of buildings)				
TOTAL RETURN-C + GROWTH	182,441	11,239	15,105	208,785
TOT AFTER TAX RET ON ASSETS	0.107	0.051	0.050	0.094
AFTER TAX DISCOUNT	0.082	0.066	0.067	0.078
NET PRESENT VALUE FOR 5 YRS	174,370	(13,262)	(20,867)	140,241

After tax disc = disc rate 3 (1 − [taxes/(taxable inc + depre)])

Since motel cash flow is on an after tax basis, the return to other possible investments also should be on an after tax basis. However, we add depreciation back into taxable income because alternative investments in financial instruments would not have depreciation to reduce taxable income.

Mary, Sally, and Jan remained torn between sentimental attachment to the Carriage House Inn and keen appreciation for the problems and risk involved in owning a motel, apartment, and office building, particularly while trying to oversee their management from a distance. They wanted to protect long time, loyal employees and return to their old home from time to time. On the other hand, the assets invested in the corporation could help supplement the sisters' current income and retirement programs and send their children through college. Numerous brokers had wanted to handle the properties, although no serious negotiations or setting of prices had occurred. Traveling to the city each month constituted a major disruption to their families and professional careers.

If they kept all or some of the businesses and appointed Robert to manage them, they agreed that the family would form a board of directors to supervise the management and make final decisions on major projects. They also agreed they would pay Robert and his wife the $90,000 they were now (1987) paying a resident supervisor plus themselves for rotating in to manage the motel.

ACCOUNTING DATA

The 1987 financial report accounting data projected for 1988 (Exhibit 1) indicated the corporation was making a good income. The trust lawyers believed they could convert the old family corporation into an S corporation to avoid double taxation (i.e. taxation of profits as corporate income and then dividends as personal income). If so, the children would pay taxes at their personal marginal rate—probably 33 percent for federal taxes in 1988 and 8 percent for state taxes. Margo, nevertheless, wondered how much income the heirs could realize if they sold the corporation and invested the proceeds in broadly based financial instruments such as mutual stock funds which had been yielding 10 to 30 percent per year in the bull market of the 80s. Also, were all the businesses making money or were gains in some off-setting losses in others?

Her managerial economics course had used a very basic value or profit maximizing model which focused on all the relevant revenues and costs of a decision. Her managerial accounting course had provided a basic accounting framework for estimating these relevant revenues and costs by segments or businesses. Thus, Margo decided to try converting the financial report accounts, used mainly for tax purposes, to managerial cost accounts both on an accrual (upper part of Exhibit 2) and cash flow basis (lower part). Once she had her electronic spreadsheet programmed she could use it for other consulting projects such as advising the family on management decisions should they decide to keep the Carriage House and other businesses.

With Robert's help she separated out the VARIABLE and UNDISTRIBUTED (or programmed) costs for the three major businesses (motel, apartments, office building) from detailed financial report accounts and other records. They could trace most of the motel's variable costs for renting a room such as maid and laundry service and a rough estimate for utilities. They could not trace out minor repairs and wear and tear costs for the rooms, however, and had to leave them in the UNDISTRIBUTED SEGMENT COST category. These latter costs contained programmed cost for management, desk clerks, advertising, and maintenance of common facilities.

Then Margo and Robert went to work on the fixed costs. DEPRECIATION came from past tax returns. They estimated that this legal depreciation for tax purposes roughly reflected the wearing out and replacement cost of the physical capital. For the MARKET VALUE OF ASSETS for each business, Margo utilized the average of appraisals the trust company appointed realtors had made using recent sales of comparable properties and construction costs.

Robert could not supply the appropriate discount rates to calculate the OPPORTUNITY COST OF ASSETS. Thus, Margo asked the trust company–appointed realtors their opinion. They said over the last several years the discount rate for economy motels had averaged around 14 percent nationally but that home mortgage rates had dropped to around 10 percent currently and the prime rate to around 9 percent. Thus, Margo used a 12 percent discount rate for the motel and 10 percent for the house converted to an office building and apartments as a rough estimate so they could go ahead and fill in the rest of the accounts.

They were able to convert the NET SEGMENT MARGIN (NSM) to taxable income, taxes, and cash flow with a few simple adjustments (bottom of Exhibit 2). They continued to assume an S corporation and used the tax rates from Exhibit 1. The lawyer handling the trust had assured her that estate taxes would remain essentially the same whether the family kept or sold any of the assets or the entire corporation. Margo and a bank accountant, Bill Wise, also experimented with various cash flow payoff measures such as return on assets, net present value over several years, and present value of the assets. This, however, required a number of assumptions about growth of the land values versus depreciation and after tax discount rates, noted on the spreadsheet.

Although the cash flow for each business and the NSM for the motel looked good, no clear decision emerged. Jan, who had some business training and knew the discount rate should contain a component for risk, felt that 12 percent was far too low. Sally added that their conservative mutual funds had been yielding nearly 20 percent for the last four years. Robert argued that the NSM should include expected growth

in the land values of the businesses. He said including this growth would show the motel could cover all its costs even with higher discount rates. Mary, who had an engineering background, pointed out that the cash flow did not include repair, renovation, and rebuilding of worn out buildings and equipment which could easily cost several hundred thousand dollars.

Margo agreed they needed better estimates of discount rates, physical depreciation, potential growth rates for land values, and even returns on broadly based financial investments. Therefore, she studied the real estate consultant's report in more detail, and talked with family members again and key informants to learn more about local market conditions. She also consulted with the bank's financial and investment experts.

COMPETITIVE ENVIRONMENT

Despite the optimism which the accounting reports generally provided, a complete analysis required estimates of future revenues and costs. These depended not only on the growth in the suburban area and entry of competitors into the market but also on the costs of maintaining and improving the land and buildings.

The apartments and house converted to an office building had adequate demand given the growth and prosperity in the area. The apartments enjoyed full occupancy with tenants who generally paid their rent on time and stayed several years. A well established real estate firm had leased the house for an office and seemed content to stay there for many years. Land values had been increasing 3 to 5 percent a year in real terms over the last 20 years as the area grew and prospered. The future, however, remained unclear. Were land values inflated now? How long might a possible recession adversely affect land values? The buildings and equipment, moreover, were aging and probably would require extensive repair in the foreseeable future. A five percent physical depreciation rate could swamp potential increases in the land values.

The motel had survived turbulent markets but now perhaps confronted even greater uncertainties. During the 1970s and early 1980s the corporation had weathered challenges from new luxury motels in the area, the oil price increases, reduced travel and inflation, and a deep recession. In spite of the national economic problems, the suburban areas had prospered. Major corporate headquarters had located within several miles while high quality housing developments and commercial growth had continued along the major artery.

As the larger, more luxurious full service motels with restaurants and indoor swimming pools moved into the general area, however, the Carriage House Inn became classified as a limited service economy motel. It provided a clean, friendly family environment, coffee, juice, and sweet rolls for breakfast, and an outdoor swimming pool in a nicely landscaped environment for an average $32 per room sold in 1987. As the mother would say, "With fewer costly frills and a virtually paid-off, low interest mortgage, we can easily underprice those new motels."

The Carriage House Inn also enjoyed a loyal clientele of repeat business representatives during the week and relatives visiting families in the local community during holidays and summer vacations. Its listing in the American Automobile Association's (AAA) guidebooks generated significant off the roads business. Although the motel was located over three miles from the nearest interstate highway and over half a mile from the nearest limited access state highway, it had enjoyed a phenomenal 83 percent occupancy rate for the last 10 to 15 years. The motel industry generally averages about 65 percent occupancy.

Nevertheless, in the later 1980s and for the 1990s the Carriage House Inn faced several new threats. Nationwide the economy motel segment was becoming overbuilt. Rumors persisted that a major motel chain was planning to build an economy motel with a restaurant at the off ramp of the limited access state highway about half a mile from the Carriage House Inn. The motel's plant and equipment were aging and within the foreseeable future might require some major renovation and style changes, which easily could cost one to two hundred thousand dollars, to keep the motel competitive. Robert's preliminary negotiations with several banks indicated they would charge about 16 percent on major renovation loans.

Nelson Ledbetter, a financial analyst with the bank, filled Margo in on the national economic situation and financial markets. Conservative financial instruments such as broadly based mutual funds and even insured savings accounts had yielded high rates of return averaging from nearly 10 to over 20 percent for the last four years. As the expansion out of the deep 1982 recession got longer, however, more economists were predicting lower consumer spending and perhaps another recession. Interest rates started moving back up in mid 1987 while oil prices, which had dropped sharply in 1986, were recovering and might increase overall inflation. These movements could adversely affect an inflated stock and bond market. Nelson pointed out that historically (1926 to 1985) Standard and Poor's index of 500 stocks had averaged almost a nominal 10 percent and real 7 percent return. He also indicated that over the last few years the bank had used about a 14 percent discount rate for small to medium sized motels like the Carriage House Inn.

Margo still remained uneasy about using discount rates to incorporate all the risk the motel faced. From her statistics courses she remembered a distinction between average and individual risk. She also wanted to estimate the impact of competition from new local economy motels on the Carriage House's occupancy rates, revenues, NSM, and cash flow. She needed some marketing research data to estimate these potential impacts.

MARKET RESEARCH DATA

Several months earlier Robert and his wife had done a survey of the Carriage House Inn's customers to see what they wanted in terms of rates, service, amenities, decor, and other motel characteristics. The motel staff had asked a cross section of guests to fill out the survey one typical week. In general the guests indicated that they were satisfied with the Carriage House. They like the clean, neat rooms, friendly family atmosphere, and the relatively low rates for the area. Many, however, were also very enthusiastic about major renovations. A number suggested putting a hot tub by the swimming pool like the larger hotels. One lady even gave extensive suggestions for new wallpaper and drape designs on the back of her questionnaire. Of course, virtually all of the guests wanted low room rates.

Although this survey supported Robert's position that the motel could remain competitive and keep its customers and high occupancy rate with major renovation, Margo remained a little uneasy. One of her marketing courses had stressed that consumers usually could not tell how they weigh product or service characteristics. Thus, more sophisticated market research studies ask consumers to rate products with different characteristics. Then the studies use these ratings to estimate the average weights customers put on the characteristics. Robert and his wife, moreover, had a vested interest in the data.

Thus, Margo asked Jim Brady, a marketing research staff member, to help her do another survey. They developed a short questionnaire asking Carriage House customers to rate the attractiveness of differ-

ent motel style-price options in the immediate area (Exhibit 3). The motel staff had about 30 representative customers fill out the questionnaire. These customers mainly represented repeat traveling sales people and persons visiting relatives in the area. Off-the-road customers traveling through the area constituted a minority of the Carriage House clients. This gave almost 100 usable ratings of different style-price combinations.

Theoretically, the average rating for each style-price combination would give a rough estimate of the occupancy for the Carriage House or a similar motel. For example, Jim calculated the average rating for the Carriage House under assumption 1 in the questionnaire (the present style-price combination with no other economy motels in the immediate area) at 9.2 out of a possible 10. This suggested that about 92 percent of the existing customers would return. The actual Carriage House Inn summer occupancy rate during the week exceeded 90 percent.

Next, Jim ran a multiple regression analysis on the data under assumption 2 in the questionnaire (a new economy motel in the area). He used RATING as the dependent variable and PRICE and STYLE as the independent variables (Exhibit 4). Both PRICE and STYLE were measured in the same units (1, 2, 3 = low, moderate, high). Thus, their coefficients indicated how heavily customers might weigh them. He used these weights to compute ratings for the Carriage House, given different combinations of STYLE and PRICE for it and its potential competitors. For example, the regression model predicted that with a new economy motel nearby, the RATING for the Carriage House would equal 5.3 (i.e., $4.7 + 2.1 (1) - 1.5 (1)$). Renovating the Carriage House, however, would raise its RATINGS, particularly if prices remained relatively low. Margo could compare these hypothetical RATINGS to the present Carriage House RATINGS (assumption 1) and

EXHIBIT 3   Questionnaire

Valued Guests:

We would appreciate your ratings of several possible motel styles and prices in this immediate area. Assuming you have the following motel options, please rate the probability you would stay in each option.

1. First assume that the present situation continues to exist with the Carriage House Inn as the only economy motel within several miles of this highway exit. The motel continues to have its same prices, service, and upkeep. How would you rate your probability of staying at the Carriage House Inn on a scale from 0 to 10 where 10—you are sure you would stay, 0—you are sure you would not stay, and 5—a fifty-fifty chance you would stay?

2. Now assume that two other economy motels exist in this immediate area near the highway exchange along with the present Carriage House. One of these motels resembles the Carriage House but has undergone major renovation and redecoration to modernize it. It has service similar to the Carriage House. The other economy motel is a new structure with a restaurant and similar quality furniture as the Carriage House but of course new. The following boxes indicate the various style-price options these motels might have. Please write a number from 0 to 10 in each box to indicate your probability of staying in a motel with that style-price combination, given the availability of the other style-price combinations listed. Use each rating number only once. Again 0—the lowest rating possible, and 5—an intermediate rating.

MOTEL STYLE-PRICE OPTIONS

AVERAGE ROOM RATE	(1) CARRIAGE HOUSE AS IT IS NOW	(2) A SIMILAR MOTEL WITH RENOVATION	(3) A NEW ECONOMY MOTEL WITH A RESTAURANT
(1) $35			
(2) $40			
(3) $45			

at least try to ascertain any possible trends in occupancy with different STYLES, PRICES, and competition.

FINAL DECISION MAKING

Margo remained somewhat bewildered with the various accounting and financial techniques and data estimates. It seemed that each technique gave a partial analysis, leaving out some key variables and not agreeing with the other techniques. Different data assumptions, moreover, led to widely different results. She finally decided to try to fall back on that very basic economic model and list all the relevant changes in total revenue and total

EXHIBIT 4   Regression Model of Motel Ratings as a Function of Style and Price

*** MULTIPLE LINEAR REGRESSION ***

DEPENDENT VARIABLE: RATING   81 VALID CASES

COEFF OF DETERM:	0.0659705	ESTIMATED CONSTANT TERM:	4.70370
MULTIPLE CORR COEFF:	0.812222	STANDARD ERR OF ESTIMATE:	1.53489

ANALYSIS OF VARIANCE FOR THE REGRESSION:

SOURCE OF VARIANCE	DEGREES OF FREEDOM	SUM OF SQUARES	MEAN OF SQUARES	F TEST	PROB
REGRESSION	2	356.241	178.120	75.6065	0.0000
RESIDUALS	78	183.759	2.35589		
TOTAL	80	540.000			

VARIANCE	REGRESSION COEFFICIENT	STANDARDIZED COEFFICIENT	STANDARD ERROR	T	PROB
STYLE	2.11111	0.667592	0.208872	10.1072	0.0000
PRICE	−1.46296	−0.462630	0.208872	−7.00411	0.0000

cost the family would experience by keeping the Carriage House Inn. She could then change data assumptions and at least range the NET SEGMENT MARGIN and perhaps other payoff measures in Exhibit 2.

First she just ranged the discount rate to account for risk. This generated a range of NET SEGMENT MARGINS for the motel. As a check she left the DISCOUNT RATE constant and ranged each possible revenue and cost category. For example, she put in a low and high occupancy rate in the spreadsheet. This generated a range of REVENUES, VARIABLE COSTS, and OPERATING CONTRIBUTION MARGINS. Next she ranged depreciation to reflect assumptions about future repair costs and possible renovations. Finally, she accounted for possible growth in land values by adding in a dollar amount to NET SEGMENT MARGIN from most pessimistic to most optimistic. If she had time, she could incorporate these ranges into the CASH FLOW and CASH FLOW PAYOFF

MEASURES. She could also utilize more formal uncertainty approaches such as that described in the text.

Questions

1. In contrast to our discussion in the textbook, this firm contains three quite distinct businesses. Is it possible to allocate all the firm's costs to one and only one of these three businesses? If not, what are the difficulties?

2. To what extent can the data in Exhibit 1 resolve the questions Margo Filmore (and the heirs) faced?

3. In Exhibit 2, why did Margo Filmore subtract the opportunity cost of assets to get the contribution of each segment of the corporation to corporate overhead and profits?

4. Which segments of the firm seem to represent a sound business investment

in terms of 1988 estimated payoffs or returns?

5. What do the expected future market environment and market research data suggest about the future competitive position of the Carriage House Inn?

6. How important in this decision are forecasts of future land values and the costs of possible major repairs?

7. Using the simulation techniques described in the text, Margo Filmore found that the probability distribution of the motel's net segment margin was as follows:

Net segment margin	Probability
Less than −$74,280	0.25
−$74,280 to −$27,720	.135
−$27,720 to $18,840	.340
$18,840 to $65,400	.340
$65,400 to $111,960	.135
$111,960 and over	.025

Interpret these results, and indicate whether—and, if so, how—they throw light on the decision to be made.

Part Eight
GOVERNMENT ACTIONS AND MANAGERIAL BEHAVIOR

CHAPTER 16

Government and Business

Chapter Profile

Commissions that regulate public utilities often set price at a level at which it equals average total cost, including a "fair rate of return" on the firm's investment. One difficulty with this arrangement is that, since the firm is guaranteed this rate of return (regardless of how well or poorly it performs), there is no incentive for the firm to increase its efficiency. Although **regulatory lag** results in some incentives of this sort, they often are relatively weak.

There has been a great deal of controversy over the practices of the regulatory commissions. Many economists have viewed them as lax or ill conceived. In many areas, like transportation, there has been a movement toward deregulation. In the airline industry, this movement has been particularly dramatic.

The socially optimal level of pollution (holding output constant) is at the point where the marginal cost of pollution equals the marginal cost of pollution control. In general, this will be at a point where a nonzero amount of pollution occurs. To establish incentives that will lead to a more nearly optimal level of pollution, the government can establish effluent fees and enact direct regulations, among other things.

In 1890, the Sherman Act was passed. It outlawed any contract, combination, or conspiracy in restraint of trade and made it illegal to monopolize or attempt to monopolize. In 1914, Congress passed the Clayton Act, and the Federal Trade Commission was created. A more recent antitrust development was the Celler-Kefauver Anti-Merger Act of 1950.

The real impact of the antitrust laws depends on the interpretation placed on these laws by the courts. In its early cases, the Supreme Court put forth and used the famous **rule of reason**—that only unreasonable combinations in restraint of trade, not all trusts, required conviction under the Sherman Act. The situation changed greatly in the 1940s when the court decided that Alcoa, because it controlled practically all of the nation's aluminum output, was in violation of the antitrust laws. In the early 1980s, two major antitrust cases—against American Telephone and Telegraph and the IBM Corporation—were decided.

The **patent laws** grant the inventor exclusive control over the use of an invention for 20 years from initial filing in exchange for his or her making the invention public knowledge. The patent system enables innovators to appropriate a larger portion of the social benefits from their innovations than would be the case without it, but they frequently have only a limited effect on the rate at which imitators appear. Nonetheless, firms continue to make extensive use of the patent system.

Foreign trade is important to all countries. It enables people in one country to purchase products that either cannot be produced there or can be produced less expensively or with higher quality elsewhere. Trade permits specialization, and specialization increases output. Differences among nations in resource endowments and in human and nonhuman resources are a major basis for specialization. Sometimes when consumers gain through decreased prices, producers in that country lose. Governments often impose tariffs or quotas to redistribute the gains.

Governments sometimes impose **price floors** or **price ceilings** on products. These are politically motivated. An example of a price floor is a minimum wage, and apartment rent control is an example of a price ceiling. Either policy can create a **deadweight loss** that decreases social welfare.

The socially optimal level of pollution (holding output constant) is at the point where the marginal cost of pollution equals the marginal cost of pollution control. An **external economy** occurs when an action taken by a firm or individual results in uncompensated benefits to others. An **external diseconomy** occurs when an action taken by a firm or individual results in uncompensated costs or harm to others. **Public goods** are those that can be consumed by one person without diminishing the amount that other people consume of it. There is also no way of preventing citizens from benefiting from public goods whether or not they contribute to the cost. The government provides these goods, such as national defense, because the market system will be unlikely to provide them in sufficient amounts.

Questions

Completion

1. Commissions often set price at the level at which it equals _____, including a fair return.

2. The government (can, cannot) _____ convict firms of violation of the antitrust laws merely by showing that the firms fixed prices or attempted to do so. The government (does, does not) _____ have to show what the effects were.

3. The Standard Oil case, decided in 1911, resulted in _____. The American Tobacco case, decided in 1911, resulted in _____. The U.S. Steel case, decided in 1920, resulted in _____. All of these cases were tried under Section _____ of the _____.

4. The IBM case alleged that IBM has had monopoly power in the market for _____. This case was tried under Section _____ of the _____.

5. While many economists favor the market _____ approach to antitrust policy, the majority favor the market _____ approach to evaluating undesirable monopolistic characteristics.

6. The market _____ shows the percentage of total sales or production accounted for by the biggest four firms.

7. The _____ outlawed any contract, combination, or conspiracy in restraint of trade and made it illegal to monopolize or attempt to monopolize.

8. At the socially optimal level, the cost of an extra unit of pollution equals the cost of _____ pollution by an extra unit.

9. Patent protection has increased imitation costs by a (larger, smaller) _____ percentage in the pharmaceutical industry than in the electronics industry.

10. The more an industry cuts down on the amount of waste it discharges, the _____ are its costs of pollution control.

11. The more untreated waste an industry dumps into the environment, the _____ the cost of pollution.

True or False

_____ 1. Because price levels have been rising in the past 40 years, most regulatory commissions use replacement cost to value a firm's assets.

_____ 2. Regulatory lag results in rewards for efficiency because, if a regulated firm is efficient, the lag automatically is reduced and profits increase.

_____ 3. A firm with a 60 percent market share frequently is permitted to go untouched by the antitrust laws, while at the same time two firms with 10 percent of a market sometimes are forbidden to merge.

_____ 4. Whether or not price fixing is illegal depends on the price fixers' share of the market; if their share is small enough, price fixing is not illegal under U.S. law.

_____ 5. If firm A acquires the stock or assets of a competing corporation, this may be illegal based on Section 7 of the Clayton Act, as amended by the Celler-Kefauver Act.

_____ 6. In recent years, horizontal mergers have often been disallowed by the courts, but all vertical mergers have been permitted.

_____ 7. The antitrust laws have as yet had no significant effect on business behavior and markets.

_____ 8. The U.S. patent laws grant the inventor exclusive control over the use of his or her invention for 30 years.

_____ 9. The patent system and the antitrust laws tend to push in opposite directions.

_____ 10. A firm's size is not necessarily a good indicator of the extent of its monopoly power.

_____ 11. National defense is not a public good.

_____ 12. In large part, environmental pollution is due to external economies.

Multiple Choice

1. It is illegal in the United States for rival firms:

   a. to agree to fix prices
   b. to restrict or pool output
   c. to share markets on a predetermined basis
   d. all of the above
   e. only a and b

2. It is illegal in the United States for a firm:

   a. to set its price equal to that of one of its competitors
   b. to merge with a larger firm
   c. to charge one customer a different price than another under any circumstances
   d. to license its patents
   e. none of the above

3. The most important reason why economists oppose monopoly is that, as compared with perfect competition, monopolies:

   a. reap higher profits
   b. charge higher prices
   c. result in a misallocation of resources
   d. are unlikely to be philanthropic
   e. none of the above

4. In the United States in 2007, what percentage of manufacturing assets were controlled by companies with assets of $1 billion or more?

   a. 85 percent
   b. 50 percent
   c. 10 percent
   d. 25 percent
   e. 99 percent

5. If firms enter into exclusive and tying contracts that substantially lessen competition, this is illegal according to the:

   a. Sherman Act, Section 1
   b. Sherman Act, Section 2
   c. Clayton Act
   d. Federal Trade Commission Act
   e. Celler-Kefauver Act

6. If a firm enters into a contract in restraint of trade, this is illegal based on the:

   a. Sherman Act, Section 1
   b. Sherman Act, Section 2
   c. Clayton Act
   d. Federal Trade Commission Act
   e. Celler-Kefauver Act

7. In 1958, the Antitrust Division sued Bethlehem Steel and Youngstown Sheet and Tube to stop a proposed merger between them. This case was brought under the:

    a. Sherman Act, Section 1
    b. Sherman Act, Section 2
    c. Robinson-Patman Act
    d. Federal Trade Commission Act
    e. Celler-Kefauver Act

8. The patent system is defended on the grounds that:

    a. it increases the incentive for invention
    b. it increases the incentive for innovation
    c. it hastens the disclosure of inventions
    d. all of the above
    e. none of the above

9. Which of the following is *not* a public good?

    a. a smog-free environment
    b. national defense
    c. blood donated to the Red Cross
    d. the Apollo space program
    e. all of the above

Problems

1. Consider an electric power plant that has the following marginal cost curve. Suppose that this plant's demand curve varies over time. For simplicity, assume that there is a peak period (when air conditioners are running and lights are on) and an off-peak period (at night). The demand curve during each period follows:

    a. Should the electric power plant charge a higher price during the peak period than during the off-peak period? Why or why not?
    b. In the 1970s, a number of regulatory commissions instituted higher rates for electric utilities during the summer than during the winter. Is this sensible, based on your answer to part a?

c. In 1978, the Public Utility Regulatory Policy Act required electric utilities to implement time-of-day pricing or to "show cause" why such pricing should not be implemented in their service areas. Time-of-day pricing calls for higher electricity rates during the times of day when the use of electricity is relatively high than during those times when it is relatively low. Does time-of-day pricing tend to promote efficiency?

2. In one of the most famous antitrust suits of this century, the government charged DuPont, the large chemical firm, with "monopolizing, attempting to monopolize and conspiracy to monopolize interstate commerce in cellophane...in violation of Section 2 of the Sherman Act." DuPont produced 75 percent of the cellophane sold in the United States.

a. Considering DuPont's share of the cellophane market, was it clear that the company was in violation of Section 2 of the Sherman Act?
b. The Supreme Court pointed out that "despite cellophane's advantage, it has to meet competition from other materials in every one of its uses....The overall result is that cellophane accounts for 17.9 percent of flexible wrapping materials." How can one tell whether cellophane had to meet competition from other materials and how stiff this competition was?
c. The Supreme Court decided that DuPont was not in violation of the Sherman Act. In reaching this decision, it pointed to the high cross elasticity of demand existing between cellophane and other flexible packaging materials like Pliofilm. Why is this of relevance?

3. In the early 1960s, the Aluminum Company of America wanted to acquire the Rome Cable Corporation, but this merger was challenged by the government. The 1958 market shares, based on alternative market definitions, are given below:

Definition	Alcoa	Rome
	(percent)	
Bare aluminum conductor wire and cable	32.5	0.3
Insulated aluminum conductor wire and cable	11.6	4.7
Combined aluminum conductor wire and cable	27.8	1.3
All bare conductor wire and cable (aluminum and copper)	10.3	2.0
All insulated conductor wire and cable	0.3	1.3
Combined insulated and bare wire and cable (all metals)	1.8	1.4

Is it obvious that the merger should have been stopped? Do you think that the courts stopped it?

4. In the early 1960s, Continental Can Company wanted to merge with the Hazel-Atlas Glass Company. Continental, the second-largest producer of tin cans in the United States, sold about one-third of all tin cans. Hazel-Atlas, the third-largest bottle maker, sold about one-tenth of all glass bottles.

Do you think that the definition of the relevant line of commerce was important in this case? Do you think that the courts prevented the merger?

5. Several firms produce a particular product. Their sales in 2001 are as follows:

Firm	Sales (millions of dollars)
A	100
B	50
C	40
D	30
E	20
F	5
G	5

   a. What is the concentration ratio in this industry?
   b. Would you regard this industry as oligopolistic? Why or why not?
   c. Suppose that firm A merges with firm G. What now will be the concentration ratio in this industry?
   d. Suppose that, after they merge, firms A and G go out of business. What now will be the concentration ratio in this industry?

6. A producer of table salt does not set the same price for all buyers. Instead, the price varies inversely and substantially with the size of the customer's order. The differences in price are not due to cost differences. The buyers are retail stores, and the large buyers can resell the salt at a lower price than can the small buyers. Is the salt manufacturer's pricing illegal? If so, what law does it violate?

7. We list a number of U.S. laws below, after which we list a number of antitrust provisions. In the blank space before each provision, put the letter corresponding to the U.S. law containing this provision.
A. Sherman Act, Section 1
B. Sherman Act, Section 2
C. Clayton Act
D. Federal Trade Commission Act
E. Celler-Kefauver Act
F. Robinson-Patman Act

     _____ a. It is illegal to enter into a contract, combination, or conspiracy in restraint of trade.
     _____ b. It is illegal to discriminate among purchasers to an extent that cannot be justified by a difference in cost.
     _____ c. It is illegal to use unfair methods of competition.
     _____ d. It is illegal to attempt to monopolize trade.
     _____ e. It is illegal to attempt to enter into exclusive and tying contracts.
     _____ f. It is illegal to attempt to discriminate among purchasers, where the effect might be to drive competitors out of business.
     _____ g. It is illegal to attempt to employ unfair or deceptive acts or practices.
     _____ h. It is illegal to attempt to acquire the stock of competing corporations.

8. Some states, such as Oregon and Vermont, have passed laws that all carbonated-beverage containers must carry a minimum refundable deposit.

   a. According to the director of communications services for American Can Company, "What *is* happening in Oregon is that consumers are paying $10 million more a year for beer and soft drinks than they did before the bottle bill became law. Retail price increases...have far exceeded those in neighboring states." Why do you think this was true?

b. According to this executive of American Can Company, "Oregon [and Vermont] consumers are denied their free choice of container." Is this true? According to William Baumol and Wallace Oates, this amounts to "a denial of...the freedom to pollute unpenalized." Do you agree?

9. According to one study of the Delaware River, the extra social costs involved in going from one level of pollution abatement to another are as follows. Also shown are the extra benefits to society in going from one level of pollution to another. (All figures are in millions of dollars.)

Transition	Extra cost	Extra benefit
From abatement level 1 to 2	35	200
From abatement level 2 to 3	20	20
From abatement level 3 to 4	130	10
From abatement level 4 to 5	245	25

a. If abatement level 1 is currently being achieved, is it socially worthwhile to advance to abatement level 2? Why or why not?

b. Is it socially worthwhile to advance to abatement level 3? Why or why not?

c. Is it socially worthwhile to advance to abatement level 4? Why or why not?

d. Is it socially worthwhile to advance to abatement level 5? Why or why not?

10. In 1965, the Ohio Valley Electric Corporation sued Westinghouse and General Electric for damages. According to Ohio Valley Electric, it had been overcharged for electrical equipment it purchased during a period when the electrical equipment producers conspired to raise prices. In the subsequent trial, it built its case in considerable part on the following graph, which shows the relationship between average order prices and book prices during 1948 to 1963.*

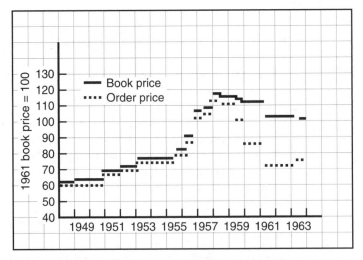

*Source: R. Sultan, *Pricing in the Electrical Oligopoly* (Boston: Harvard University, 1974).

a. The book price was the published price issued by General Electric and other electrical equipment producers. The average order price was the average price actually negotiated for such equipment. Does it appear that this equipment was frequently sold below its book price?

b. There was evidence that the electrical equipment producers had held meetings to control prices before 1959. Is the relationship between average order price and book price different in the post-1959 period than in the earlier years?

c. According to the Ohio Valley Electric Corporation, in the absence of a conspiracy, the actual order price would have borne the same relationship to the book price in the early 1950s as in the early 1960s. Specifically, it would have been about 75 percent of the book price. Is this necessarily true?

11. The overwhelming majority of families in the United States have television sets.

a. For these families, is a television program a nonrival good? That is, can one consumer enjoy this good without other consumers getting less of it?

b. Is it possible for firms to exclude some of these families from viewing certain programs?

c. Who pays for ordinary TV programs?

d. Must there be any commercials on "pay TV"?

12. "Public goods have marginal costs of zero. In other words, they can be provided as cheaply for one as for all. Consequently, it is foolish to attempt to compare the benefits of public goods with their costs. Any public good is worth producing because it benefits so many people." Comment and evaluate.

13. Assume that a country with closed borders has 100 working-age individuals. There are two options for employment within the country: fishing and working in the factory. The monthly wage at the factory equals \$2,000 and the monthly wage for fishing is $P = 4000 - 40B$, where B refers to the number of boats actively fishing. Assume further that only one person can occupy a boat.

a. Given the factory wage, how many people would work in the factory and how many would fish?

b. What is the town's total income given your answer to part a?

c. What is the optimal number of fisherman?

d. If the optimal number of fishermen fish, what is the town's income?

Answers

Completion
1. average total cost   2. can, does not   3. dissolution of Standard Oil, dissolution of American Tobacco, acquittal, 2, Sherman Act   4. electronic computers, 2, Sherman Act   5. performance, structure   6. concentration ratio   7. Sherman Act   8. reducing   9. larger   10. greater   11. greater

True or False
1. False   2. False   3. True   4. False   5. True   6. False   7. False   8. False   9. True   10. True   11. False   12. False

Multiple Choice
1. d   2. e   3. c   4. a   5. c   6. a   7. e   8. d   9. c

Problems

1. a. Many economists favor such a pricing policy. One advantage is that it would help to even out the amount of electricity utilized at various periods of time.
   b. Yes, if the demand for electric power is greater in the summer than in the winter.
   c. Yes.

2. a. No, because it was not clear that cellophane alone was the relevant line of commerce.
   b. One relevant measure is the cross elasticity of demand between cellophane and other flexible packaging materials.
   c. Because it indicates how closely these other materials can substitute for cellophane.

3. It was not obvious. The Supreme Court ruled against the merger, whereas the district court permitted it.

4. The district court said cans and bottles were separate lines of commerce, but the Supreme Court emphasized the competition between cans and bottles. The Supreme Court ruled against the merger.

5. a. 220/250 = 88 percent.
   b. Yes, because the concentration ratio is so high.
   c. 90 percent.
   d. 140/145 = 97 percent.

6. Yes. The Robinson-Patman Act.

7. a. A
   b. C
   c. D
   d. B
   e. C
   f. F
   g. D
   h. E

8. a. Because of increased costs of handling, sorting, washing, returning, and refilling bottles, according to this executive.
   b. The issue is too complex to permit a very brief answer, but many economists would agree with Baumol and Oates.

9. a. Yes, because the benefit exceeds the cost.
   b. No, because the benefit does not exceed the cost.
   c. No, because the benefit does not exceed the cost.
   d. No, because the benefit does not exceed the cost.

10. a. Yes.
    b. Yes.
    c. No. For example, increased competition among electrical equipment producers could result in a decrease in the ratio of actual order price to book price.

11. a. Yes, because once the program is put on the air, an extra family can watch it without depriving others of the opportunity to do so. In other words, once the program is broadcast to some viewers, others can watch it at no (or trivial) extra cost.

    b. Yes. A means has been devised to "scramble" the signal so that, unless a viewer's TV set is equipped to unscramble it, the viewer cannot get the program. Viewers rent this equipment or operate it by means of coins. This is called "pay TV."

    c. Advertisers pay for the broadcasts in order to air their commercials. In addition, listeners pay something, if they don't like commercials!

    d. No, because the viewers pay directly for the broadcasts.

12. It is not true that any public good is worth producing. The efficient output of a public good can be determined by summing the individual demand curves vertically and by finding the intersection with the supply curve. In many instances, the efficient output may be zero.

13. a. 50 people would fish and 50 people would work in the factory. Setting the wage of the factory as the decision point as to fish or not to fish yields

$$2,000 = 4,000 - 40B$$
$$40B = 2,000$$
$$B = 50$$

That is, 50 boats—leaving 50 individuals to work in the factory.

    b. $200,000 = 50 • $2,000 + 50 • $2,000.

    c. 25. Note that total fishing income is the price a boat can earn multiplied by the number of boats $= 4,000B - 40B • B$. The marginal revenue of a given boat is therefore $4,000 - 80B$. It follows that the optimal number of boats is set by solving

$$2,000 = 4,000 - 80B$$
$$80B = 2,000$$
$$B = 25$$

    d. $225,000. Note that the price to fish has now increased to $3,000 = 4,000 - 40 • 25$ so that

$$\$225,000 = 25 • \$3,000 + 75 • \$2,000$$

Credits